TEAMWORK
Your Key to Exponential Growth

> **Impressions, Comments and Reviews**

I have gone through the book from one end to another and must say that I have benefited a lot. I would add, that this book is a must for all Corporate Houses, big or small, where more than two persons are employed. Written in simple style, it is easy to grasp and more than that, easier to follow. On the eve of a new dawn on literary field, I salute you sir, as the rising star.

Joginder Singh
well known author and former director, CBI, India.

The book is so well written – simple, yet engrossing - that I did not put it down till I finished it - a very rare phenomenon with management books and me. After having read the book, I cannot help but quote.
"Alone we can do little; together we can do so much." - Hellen Keller

B. Sunanda
Book Club India

A special mention must be made of the distinctive manner in which the book takes us through the lessons of life using the platform - journey of the protagonist, Raj.
Life needs such doses of positive energy and this certainly ranks Up there. Some things in life need reinforcement and this book leaves a lasting imprint.

Srinivas Rangarajan

The book is well written. The concept of **win-win-win** situation has added a new dimension to the interpersonal relationship which traditionally looked only for a win- win where the ultimate beneficiary was forgotten.

Suresh Nair

Amazing. The way you convey message through story telling is that makes reading interesting. Good job done. Simple sentences with loaded meanings. One hardly finds books written in simple language these days. Hats off for the wonderful book. It is my desire that your next book should be on Grit and Determination which are essential requirements of success in any field.

P.R. Balan

Thanks a ton for giving such a fantabulous content to read, absorb and use.

Roshan Khadye,
CEO, estationary

The dry topic was presented very well... Its nice refresher and adequately supported with examples and most catchy were the little sketches...

S.N. Krishna

My compliments to you for sharing such wonderful thoughts through your book and unfolding the "KEY TO SUCCESS" that everyone and anyone can use to achieve his own dreams.
I find some of the thoughts that you have shared in your book can spark instantaneous inspiration in a person reading the book and can put him into a positive action.

Ashok Vasandani
CMD, Minar Management

TEAMWORK

Your Key to
Exponential Growth

S Kumar

STERLING PAPERBACKS
An imprint of
Sterling Publishers (P) Ltd.
A-59, Okhla Industrial Area, Phase-II, New Delhi-110020.
Tel: 26387070, 26386209; Fax: 91-11-26383788
E-mail: mail@sterlingpublishers.com
www.sterlingpublishers.com

Teamwork: Your Key to Exponential Growth
© 2012, S Kumar
ISBN 978 81 207 6322 7
First Edition : October 2011
Reprint : February 2012

All rights are reserved.
No part of this publication may be reproduced, stored in a retrieval system or transmitted, in any form or by any means, mechanical, photocopying, recording or otherwise, without prior written permission of the author.

Printed in India
Printed and Published by Sterling Publishers Pvt. Ltd., New Delhi-110 020.

This book is dedicated to
all my family members,
my dearest friends and
all my colleagues,
my past and present TEAM
because of whom
I am here
TODAY!

Gratitude

My humble obeisance to the almighty, the creator, for allowing me to do the little things that I am capable of in this lifetime and be a part of his TEAM.

My gratitude to all GURUS and MENTORS, who have pushed me selflessly to perform and wished to see me successful.

Every great soul right from my Ashaan (my first guru from village) who held my tiny fingers and helped me write the first letters on sand, to Dr.Shweta and Dr. Vikram who taught me the finer things about presentations using the latest technologies. Above all for believing in me that I could complete this book.

To all the teachers who came in between for a season and a reason.

To Anju Sharma who readily agreed to support my writings with her sketches.

To all those 500+ speakers from around the world who touched a chord in me and inspired me time and again.

To all those wonderful writers who boosted my confidence and lifted me time and again.

To the entire team at Sterling Publishers for their excellent support, especially Sonia Saini for the patience shown in proof reading and editing.

And finally, I have to mention the unconditional support and guidance provided by Ammavan (uncle) Mr. Pappadi Ramachandran Nair, leading up to this book and through it.

My salute to you all!

Contents

Chapter 1
Meeting a Millionaire 1

Chapter 2
Change and Adapt 10

Chapter 3
Importance of Preparation 25

Chapter 4
Communicate to Develop Relationships 45

Chapter 5
Commit with a Selfless Attitude 58

Chapter 6
Focus on the Mission of Your Organisation 70

Chapter 7
Collaborate for Multiplying Results 79

Chapter 8
Master the Never-Say-Die Attitude 92

Chapter 1

Meeting a Millionaire

The SUV rolled and came to a smooth halt next to my car. As I waited for the traffic signal to turn green, I could not help but look admiringly at the gentle beast waiting next to me. I had been noticing the vehicle through my rear-view mirror as I approached the traffic light. The shining metallic ivory colour (white diamond as it is known), the 22 inches alloy wheel, the grand Cadillac logo on the front were all quite a sight. My gaze slowly shifted to the person driving the Cadillac escalade. There was something about the vehicle and the way it was being driven. There was a positive aura around the driver and the grand vehicle he was driving. The driver looked in no hurry and he appeared to be enjoying every moment of his drive, tapping his fingers on the steering wheel probably listening to some Bollywood number. It was a strange feeling; I could feel myself surrounded by a positive energy field. There was a subtle smile on the face of the driver and he looked cool and in total command. The signal turned green and I took a right turn to my apartment complex at the junction, but I kept looking at the Cadillac moving towards the I395 (interstate highway) until it vanished towards Washington side.

Thirty seconds were enough for me to register the calm and composed face of the driver. Days passed by but the aura of the driver still lingered in my thoughts. I went about my daily chores without much change in routine. Job, family and social commitments everything was the same until I met him again. And my life changed — positively for me.

It was at the birthday party of Rohit's 6-year-old daughter. The party was being held at the community hall inside their residential complex. It was spacious enough for about two hundred people. Rohit and his wife had invited only close friends and relatives, but due to the long weekend most people had travelled out of state so there wasn't much of a crowd; just about 30 odd families. Rohit's daughter Priyanka was playing with her friends, and there were children running all around. I noticed a small crowd at the far end of the hall, quite jubilant and having a good time. As I approached the crowd I could not believe my eyes but there he was; he was talking delightedly to a small group that had surrounded him. As I started walking towards them, Rohit joined me. He put an arm around me and asked, "Have you met Raj?"

I replied with a question: "Raj? Are you talking about the guy who owns that chain of restaurants in and around Washington?"

"Yeah the same guy. I am sure you are aware that he landed in the United States with just four dollars and sixty cents, and today his net worth is about Hundred million US dollars. His monthly income is apparently over $100,000," said Rohit.

My Indian mind set to work immediately. "Dude, that is about forty-five lakh (4.5 million) Indian rupees a month. Hey I don't make that in a year. It would be a pleasure to meet such a successful person. Now don't you tell me that Raj is here."

"Oh sure he is here. See that charming guy in the white half-sleeved shirt and crisp khaki pants, that's him. Come I will introduce you to him," said Rohit.

As we started moving towards Raj I couldn't help but admire his dressing sense. He was wearing tan leather shoes along with a matching belt. Even the strap of his watch was of the same tan colour. He was also wearing glasses with a golden Cartier frame. All his accessories were tastefully matched. Undoubtedly, he was the best dressed man in the entire crowd.

I could not believe what I had just heard. "You mean this is Raj, the guy whom the Indians respect in Washington DC area"? "Wow!" is all that I could say as Rohit dragged me towards the small crowd.

I was in total admiration of this man and wished to learn from his experience and hear about his success mantra. Rohit introduced me to Raj and told him that I was relatively new in America and that, though, I worked for a living my passion was writing. Following this short introduction, I too joined the conversation. The buffet table was being set and everyone left to assist leaving behind Raj, Rohit and me. I grabbed the opportunity to ask Raj if he could share some of his life-changing experiences with me. He said he was willing to but that he would be free only after two weeks and was flying out to Paris the next morning to attend a seminar and exhibition on food and beverages. We exchanged numbers and he promised to meet me a week later.

Two weeks flew by in a jiffy. Raj had asked me to meet him at his office, which was above his famous restaurant on a busy street in downtown DC (District of Columbia). As downtown DC is known for its lack of parking space, I decided to take the metro instead. I reached his office at the appointed time of 2.30 in the afternoon. Just outside his office door, a bronze idol in a *Namaste* pose welcomed me. Inside I was greeted by a charming Raj, who himself opened the office door for me. I was expecting the office to be a swanky plush one but it turned out to be a simple but a stylishly spacious one. On one side was a 3+2 sofa set with a centre table, and on the wall behind the sofa hung an aristocratic painting in an expensive golden Italian frame. Later on during our talk Raj mentioned it was a replica of a 19th century painting by Raja Ravi Varma. On the other end of the office was a large walnut-coloured office table with matching chairs. We decided to settle on the comfortable sofa and Raj offered to get me tea. Raj was simply dressed but neatly turned out. He sat with a subtle smile on his face, which by now had become synonymous with him. As we settled down I could not help but notice his eagerness to know more about me, my background, about how had I landed up in the United States and such things. I had come to visit him seeking and wanting to know more about his success mantra, but instead he seemed to be more eager to know about me. Intending to show interest in the person one is talking to, I asked him, "Raj I would like to know how you carved your path to success; tell me everything if you will or better give me just that one secret pill that I and other hard working people can use to succeed".

Raj's reply broke my heart.

"Look dude there is nothing like a secret pill that you can take and succeed".

"Then", I could hardly muster enough courage to speak.

"Yes," he said, "there is definitely a formula for success and you can use it to succeed and succeed the way you want. Looking back, there wasn't any strategy that I systematically followed. I merely went about doing what I liked most. There was a burning desire in me to succeed. If at all we need to put everything into one pill, then we could say that one needs to move from point A to point B and then from B to C."

"What are points A, B and C. Is it an acronym", I asked curiously. "Not exactly," said Raj. "A is the position I was comfortable in like most people — active yet not very productive; they like to be independent B is being bonded to the team they are supportive; and C is creative. ."

After a thoughtful pause he said, "Working for myself made me extremely happy, neither taking interest in seeking anyone's help nor ready to help anyone. That feeling did not last for long when I found that people around me were moving ahead fast and they were a lot happier than me. It did not take me long to realise that even though I had enough potential like them, I was unable to exploit my potential fully.

I was shocked when I realised that I was utilising a mere 20 to 30 percent of my potential."

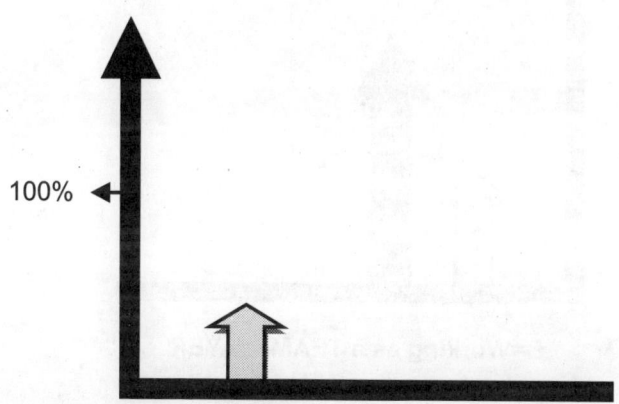

A= Independent; working in ISOLATION

"I had to make a choice; I could either blame everyone and everything for my failures and troubles or accept reality and then earnestly do something to improve my situation. Obviously it wasn't a comfortable decision, but one has to do what it takes to move on in life. I started slowly and steadily on the path, by watching successful people who had achieved and moved on in life. Focusing on others' achievements inspired me. It was a pleasure to watch such people at work. These individuals not only enjoyed their own work but also helped their teammates with their work as they went about accomplishing their own tasks. Their attitude was entirely different from mine and they displayed more of a positive mentality. That is when I realised that that's how TEAM PLAYERS behave and that this is what helps them accomplish more. It was then that I made the decision to gel and bond with my team and consequently move on to position 'B' and become a team player. In no time my performance went from a mere 20–30 percent to about 90 percent, almost tripling my accomplishments."

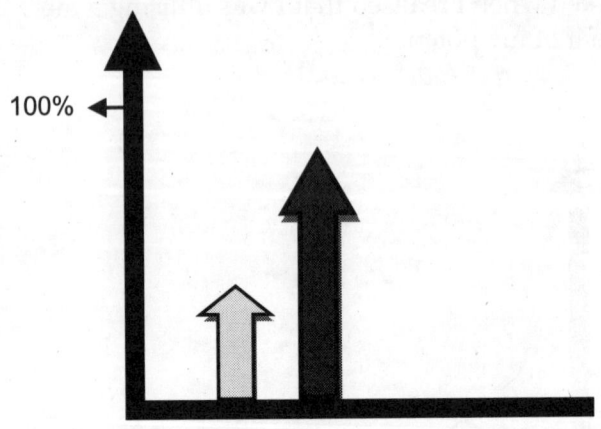

B=Working as a TEAMPLAYER

"Wow, you tripled your accomplishments just by bonding with a team", I said in amazement.

"Yes, a true TEAMPLAYER can reach 90 to 95 percent of their potential just by actively associating with a TEAM. By shifting from the self-centered attitude to focusing on others led to tripling my accomplishments."

Here I interrupted him and questioned, "So, was it at position 'C' where you achieved all your success?"

"Exactly" he said and complimented me for getting it right.

"Is there a position 'D' too?" I asked again giving into my impatience.

"Yes of course. 'D' is being destructive and a sure death, in this lifetime there is nothing after death. This happens when everyone turns against you, by working against you. At times it is difficult to face the deadly challenge posed by a force of collective people either physically or emotionally. Especially, in a workplace if everyone turns against you, you go down that never-ending downward spiral. You lose precious time, energy and money, and even to think of a new beginning takes substantial time. Dude don't even think of 'D'; it is not worth wasting this precious life on getting everyone to work against you."

"Yes indeed," I said, "Please tell me about 'C'."

"Well 'C' is the position where you are creative and charged. You work in such a fashion that everyone you know starts to wish you well and work for your success directly or indirectly. You achieve astounding success by reaching more than 200 times your potential. This is the position everyone should strive to achieve. If you are happy at position 'B' wait till you taste success at position 'C'."

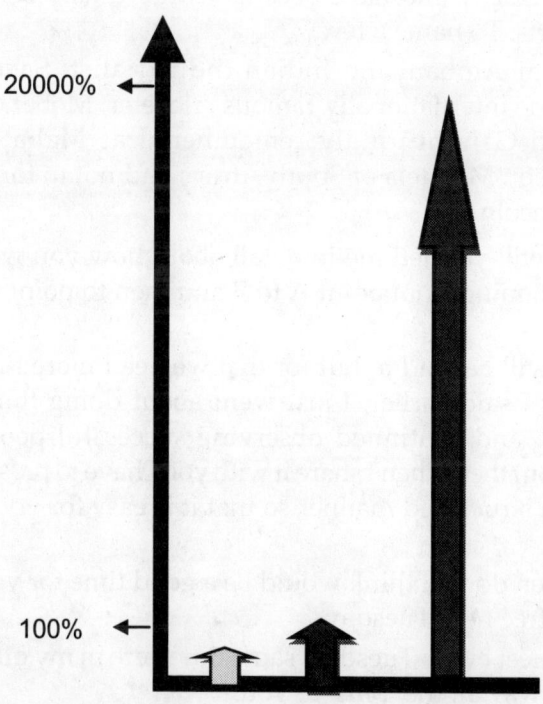

C=Creative, when everyone works towards your success

"One name that comes to my mind instantly" said Raj "is that of Amitabh Bacchhan, the legend of Indian cinema. The Indian movie industry churns out more than 900 films a year, which is approximately a minimum of three movies a day. And then there are thousands of actors, but Amitabh Bacchhan is probably the only Indian actor who is equally revered nationally and internationally. He is one person whom you can pinpoint and say that here is the person who has achieved more than 200 times his individual potential. If you look at his acting skills there are many actors who do an equally good job but then what did he do extra that catapulted him to become the Numero Uno. Likewise, there are many ordinary individuals who have achieved multi-folds their individual capacity and have become extraordinary solely by their efforts. To name a few:

Dhirubhai Ambani the Indian industrialist; Sachin Tendulkar, the internationally famous cricketer; Mohandas Karamchand Gandhi fondly remembered as Mahatma Gandhi; Nelson Mandela of South Africa; and not to forget Abraham Lincoln."

"So Raj, will you tell me in detail about how you went about transitioning from point A to B and then to point C," I asked.

"Sure, I will be glad to but for that we need more time; moreover as I said earlier, I just went about doing things I liked to do and continued observing successful people around me. But then when I share it with you I have to present it to you in a structured manner so that it is easy for you to follow."

"Raj, when do you think would be a good time for you? Will you be free next Tuesday?"

"Let us meet every Tuesday, same time here in my office until I give away all the 'pills' to you."

We both had a hearty laugh and I bid goodbye to Raj with a promise to meet him next Tuesday.

Individual Achievement Chart

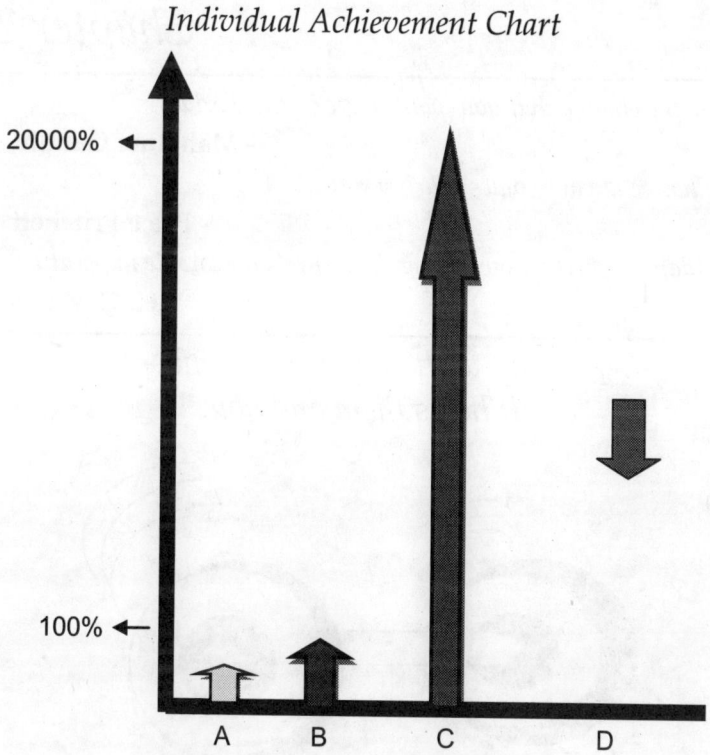

A=Independent; working in isolation
B=Supportive; working as a TEAMPLAYER
C=Creative; when everyone works toward your success
D=Destructive; when everyone works against you

> *Like water, adjust yourself in any situation, in any shape, and most importantly always find your own way.*
>
> **- Anonymous**

Chapter 2

> *Be the change that you want to see in the world*
> **- Mahatma Gandhi**
>
> *Change always comes bearing gifts.*
> **- Price Pritchett**
>
> *Adapt or perish, now as ever, is nature's inexorable imperative.*
> **- H. G. Wells**

Keep up with your team members.
It helps them and you.

Rotating at different speeds of 10 kms and 20 kms on the same axel the wheels will move in a circular motion.

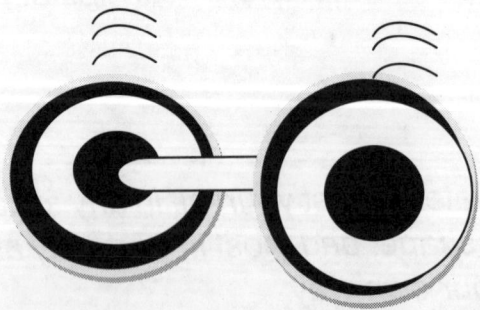

Both wheels rotating at 20 kms will help the wheels go in a forward motion. This will happen even if the speeds of both the wheels are 1 km.

Change and Adapt

As agreed the previous Tuesday, we met again in Raj's office in downtown DC and after exchanging pleasantries we got down to business.

Raj continued from where he had stopped last time. "In those initial days, after I migrated to the US, I had started doing odd jobs. I worked in a restaurant to support myself, and I also joined a university to continue my education. At first the education was an excuse to get a student visa so that I was legal in this country, but the education boosted my confidence and improved my communication skills. My etiquettes too began to improve and so did my outlook towards life. At the restaurant I worked for 20 hours a week; I had started with clearing and cleaning tables to washing plates. The work did not dishearten me a bit as I knew it was a temporary phase and it would pass. But I was not happy inside and I felt I could do better. When I compared myself to others, I realised I was a lot talented than most of them. But the most important thing that I noticed was that I did not complain about the job nor did I refuse to do what I was asked to do by my supervisor.

One day the assistant chef did not turn up and I was asked to stand in. I am a foodie; I love cooking and so

> It is a futile exercise to try and change others, and quite frustrating too. There cannot be a more rewarding experience than changing ourselves.

I grabbed the opportunity. The owner was extremely happy with that day's work — no untoward incident had occurred in the kitchen. The next day when I reported for work, the owner asked me if I would like to work in the kitchen assisting the chef. He also added that he would pay me an extra dollar per hour if I opted for the new job. I grabbed it with both hands as I would straightaway make an extra $80 more per month. The chef too liked me as I was of good help to him. I worked with him for about six months and he taught me the preparation of many of the dishes. I did not realise that I was graduating to be a finer chef under his guidance. Then one Wednesday afternoon, when we had closed after the lunch-hour rush, my owner sat with me to have lunch. I still remember every second of that conversation as my life was about to change, big time."

As he took a spoonful of *dahi bhaath* (yoghurt and rice) from his plate he looked at me and said,

"Raj I am opening a new restaurant in Maryland. Your master tells me that you have evolved into a fine chef and so I would like you to be the chef of my new restaurant."

He also added that he would sponsor me and would at first pay me $2500 a month and also that I could move into the company guest house near the restaurant. I was speechless for some time because I had been struggling to make both ends meet. I was making $520 from the restaurant and another $250 by working 10 hours a week at a gas station. It took some time for me to gather myself and say an emphatic 'yes' to him.

Raj went silent for a few minutes as he was probably feeling nostalgic. He had a sentimental look on his face and I could see his eyes moisten. I cleared my throat and asked him, "Raj, what did you exactly do to move from position A to position B?"

Raj adjusted himself on the couch eager to share his wisdom with me. His facial expressions changed and he looked more prophetic when he started speaking again.

"The first thing I did was to accept the change and then accordingly change my thinking and adapt to my new atmosphere. I realised that every organisation has its own identity and character; every department or division within that organisation has its own identity and character; and of course every individual in that department has his or her own identity and character. When each individual in that department sheds that individual identity and character and takes on the identity of the department for the benefit of the organisation, it is then one truly becomes a TEAM PLAYER. For this I had to change my thinking and the way I acted on my thinking. I had to change and adapt.

Change is a must for growth:

You cannot grow without changing. If you need to change everything, do that. The reason why people do not grow is that they do not like changes. They get into a comfort zone. Change is uncomfortable, but as you move ahead you will realise the rewards that are in store for you. Sometimes you may have to change a lot of things surrounding you, especially the people who obstruct your growth. Move away from the people who obstruct your growth and get new friends and people who will support you or play neutral. Sometimes you may need to change your habits, the way you dress, what you eat and drink. At times a whole new makeover would be required. If your current situation is not helping you, try changing to adapt to the new situation. It might bring huge rewards.

It is a futile exercise to try and change others and is quite frustrating too. There cannot be a more rewarding experience than changing ourselves. Be wise and do not make people jealous as you grow, though that is not within your control; but, what I mean is, do not add fuel to their jealousy. Growth is the time when you need all the prayers and blessings of people. Good wishes and prayers are required when you are down and out, when you are growing, and when you reaching the pinnacle and want to happily stay there. In a nutshell, you need prayers and good wishes of everyone all the time. I once read that even an enemy or your competitor has to bless you if you have to win against them. Change to fit into the team then adapt to be a part of the team and contribute your talent generously to the team.

Change is inevitable:

Every nanosecond our body is changing, and to optimise our performance we need to constantly keep updating new and improved information in our brain. This will help us to seek positive thoughts and improve our attitude to a great extent. Opportunity visits us all the time but is disguised! A person willing to change and adapt always recognises it and acts on it. Change brings new opportunities and choices that then produce even more demanding challenges. In fact, every living form of God's creation keeps changing. Even a small seed that germinates into a plant keeps changing as it grows. It does not even move from its place yet it keeps changing. It sheds its old leaves as it grows new leaves. It develops new branches and soon turns into a gigantic tree. Why are we humans so unyielding to change in our lives? Is it because of some fear — the fear of the unknown ahead of us? FEAR as it is said is nothing but False Evidence Appearing Real. The only logical remedy to tackle FEAR is action.

> Change to fit in; then adapt to be part of the team; followed by a generous contribution of your talent to the team.

Do you dread to pick up that phone and make a call to your prospect? Do you fear to give that first smile or extend your hand to shake hand with a stranger? Just go ahead and do it and you would be amazed at the relaxed feeling after you have attempted what you have been dreading to do before.

Anxiety before attempting anything new is natural. But let it not bog you down so much that you become inactive. Everyone goes through the shivers. Even experienced people get that fear for a while, but with time they have

> F - False
> E - Evidence
> A - Appearing
> R - Real

learned that this fear is momentary and so they go ahead and accomplish their task. Accept change by displaying patience and understanding. If you get tense or panicky it is bound to complicate things. Rather, approach it lightheartedly. Breathe deep, take it easy and contemplate how to make the best out of your new opportunity that has presented itself disguised in front of you. Have you not heard the age old saying, 'turn every obstacle into an opportunity'? Develop that attitude to face challenges. Every challenge you refuse to face will be replaced with a bigger one in future. So just go ahead and grab the bull by the horns.

Moreover, if you look around you will notice how everything is changing. Everything, from the way we respond to the way we work has gone through humongous changes. For instance, look at the cell phone we use each day. By the time we've mastered how to use the one we own, a new one hits the market. There is simply no settling time.

Raj got up from the couch and walked up to his filing cabinet. He sifted through some folders and pulled out a photograph. He walked back to the couch where I was sitting and handed to me before settling down in front of me. It was a picture of a young funky man with shoulder length hair, an uneven and unkempt beard, smoking to his heart's content with a mischievous smile on his face. I looked at the unimpressive picture and then I saw a resemblance of the person sitting opposite me.

I exclaimed loudly, "Oh my gosh! Is this you Raj, I can't believe my eyes. What a transformation! Look at you now, neatly cropped hair, crisply dressed, clean shaven, not to talk about your infectious innocent smile".

Raj continued, "This was the change I had to work on to bring within me, internally and externally. It was not easy, because I loved the wild life — long hair, un-groomed appearance, late night parties smoking and the like. I had to make a tough choice; did I want this wild lifestyle, which was anyway not doing anything good to me or my image or did I want to change myself to succeed in life. I am glad I decided to quit my wild life and become sober.

Yes Raj, we all are delighted as much as you are about your success.

Raj smiled and continued...

Begin with what you have:

You need to leave point A to reach point B. It is impossible to tread towards point B by still being focused on A. Focus on your new goal, your new target and develop that burning desire to achieve or acquire what you have set forth to do. Begin with what you have; you don't have to wait to be perfect to begin the task at hand. Begin with what you have, and begin by moving from where you are. As you go along you will develop the skills and knowledge required to accomplish the task in hand. When you develop that giving attitude (if you have been hoarding so far) you automatically develop a magnetism that attracts people towards you. People love to associate with result-oriented and successful people. As people gather around you to help you in whatever way they can, you get that much needed fuel to surge ahead. This gives birth to vigour, enthusiasm

> Every nanosecond our body is changing and to optimise our performance we need to constantly keep updating new and improved information in our brain.

and courage; it increases your confidence and helps you accomplish your task at hand much easier and faster.

Learn as you go along:

Learn from every source possible. Learn from everyone; encourage ideas coming from associates and juniors too. Sometimes valuable information that might help you surge ahead can come from the most unlikely of sources. Keep the door open to learning at all times. A closed mind cannot function.

> Every challenge you refuse to face at present will be replaced by a bigger one in the future.

Take the instance of a parachute. A parachute works only when it is open. You learn by either reading, listening or by associating. Develop that insatiable hunger for knowledge. Gather information as to what extra knowledge will help you in your current job or passion that you are pursuing. Invest in learning new skills. If you are not into the habit of reading it will not be easy to develop that habit but it certainly is not an impossible task.

Here is an easy way; start by reading fifteen minutes a day continuously for about three weeks. Do not go to bed if you have not read that day. Make it a system that you follow religiously. Initially start reading light material — stuff that makes you happy. There is no harm even if you start with Tintin comics or articles from magazines. Don't give a damn about what the world is reading. Begin somewhere with something and let the newfound interest and knowledge grow on you slowly. Gradually a point will come where you will be able to read substantially. I read in an article that Bill Clinton used to read close to 300 books a year while he served as the president of the United States of America — undoubtedly the busiest and toughest job on earth.

If you read the biography of most achievers and leaders, they all had one trait in common — they were all readers. It is aptly said that 'All leaders are readers'. The bigger the leader you are, the higher the number of books you have to read.

Light can invade darkness but darkness can never ever invade where there is light. Knowledge similarly removes ignorance. Knowledge is light and ignorance is darkness. Wherever there is God, evil has no place but evil can be vanquished by God. You are aware about *Diwali*, the festival of lights in India. It is celebrated all across the country by almost everyone, irrespective of the faith they follow, to mark the victory of virtue over evil, victory of knowledge over ignorance, and of course in remembrance of Lord Rama's return to his kingdom Ayodhya after completing his 14-year exile.

So illuminate your life with as much knowledge as possible. Gain more and more knowledge and then apply it to gain more benefit from it. Gain knowledge, apply it, achieve your goal, and surge ahead and then gain some more knowledge for more growth. Make this as a continuous process throughout your life. This is one asset for which you will not need a theft insurance or need to worry about losing. Attend as many training programs, seminars, workshops, exhibitions which will help you boost your knowledge as you continue reading and gaining knowledge. For knowledge once gained remains with you throughout.

Get a mentor:

A budding talent with a mentor is like a piece of gold in the hands of a goldsmith who later turns it into fine jewellery to be adored by the world. The piece of jewellery goes through torching and beating to take the shape of fine jewellery; likewise a disciple goes through a gruelling time during his preparation phase. So

> Light can invade darkness, but darkness can never ever invade where there is light. Knowledge is light and ignorance is darkness.

once you prepare yourself under the able eyes of a mentor, then it is your time to shine in this beautiful world.

We all have blind spots similar to those of vehicles. These blind spots are not visible to us but they are to our coach, mentor or our sincere well wishers. Get a mentor who could help you bring out your best and help you shine. Once you identify a mentor and seek help, surrender unconditionally, forgo your ego. Only a submissive student can unlearn and then learn from the guru.

An important factor to be kept in mind while choosing a mentor is that they should either have what you are looking for or should have the capability to help you in achieving your goal. Another step is to move on to a better-informed mentor once you have achieved what your current mentor has been helping you achieve. During your school days you, mostly, had different teachers as you advanced your grades, even for the same subject. My pre-primary teacher was not the one who taught me in primary school and definitely it was a different teacher in high school, not to tell you about my college lecturers. As you surge ahead you will need a mentor of higher expertise, experience and intelligence. So certainly we need to upgrade our mentors too.

Think Creatively:

A good Team Player is always creative. Whenever anything untoward happens, they always come up with a brilliant idea. They will never let the workflow stop. Sometimes things do not happen the way they are planned, and if you are stuck with just one way of accomplishing your task it can endanger the mission. I remember an incident my friend once narrated to me. She was working for a multinational organisation, which was celebrating its 25th year in business. An enormous hall was booked for the function. Among the 3000 odd invitees, there were celebrities, senior bureaucrats, other dignitaries and a state minister as well. The celebration was to begin by lighting a traditional lamp. VIPs including the state minister and four other celebrities were to come up on stage to light the lamp. To welcome the guest on the stage some cute young girls in white fairy frocks stood near the steps leading to the podium, with each one of them holding a small tray with floral decoration with a tiny lamp in the centre of the tray.

My friend who was the master of the ceremony, invited the VIPs onto the stage to light the traditional lamp and inaugurate the function. Under normal circumstances, a volunteer hands over a lighted candle and the VIPs light the wick and pass the candle to the next dignitary to do the same. As my friend invited the VIPs onto the stage the volunteer who was supposed to hand the lighted candle to the VIPs was suddenly nowhere in sight. He seemed to have vanished from the scene. My friend's attendant who was standing near the little girls to guide them onto the stage saw the major disaster in waiting. He immediately grabbed a bundle of candles and placed one candle each on the decorated trays and told the little girls to place themselves by the side of each dignitary and lift the trays towards them so they could take a candle each and light it from the small lamp they had in the tray.

As the cute angels walked onto the stage followed by the VIPs it was a glittering and touching sight; much less monotonous than the way they had planned earlier. When the VIPs took the candle from the tray and lighted it from the lamp even they had the best smile on their faces. The entire lights in the hall were turned off and only the stage light was focused onto the lamp and the surrounding people. My friend says it was a sight to be seen to be believed. In the earlier plan the young girls would walk first onto the stage followed by the VIPs and the young girls would disappear to the far end of the stage.

By acting in a reflex the junior employee not only salvaged the situation but actually improvised on the situation. And it was one of the best highlights of the event. When my friend later came up on stage she shared the incident and thanked the attendant. Later on, as every speaker came up to speak they individually complimented him for his presence of mind. I later got to know from my friend that the organisation helped the boy with his basic education and he was promoted to a clerical grade.

It is a good idea to participate in brainstorming sessions. Come up with new ideas and constantly contribute towards brainstorming sessions of your team. If your team does not have brainstorming sessions propose one."

Serving Mentality:

You are the servant of your Team. This is a tough sentence and if you can digest it then you do have a great future. Surrender your ego and take up the challenge to be available for the team at any point of time. You must have heard that there is no 'I' in the word 'TEAM'. Serve relentlessly without wanting to be recognised for your effort. Do your part and find time to assist other members of your team who need help. A giving attitude is always rewarding in the long run. Focus on the team's interest rather than on yours. Ultimately, it is the team effort that will bring the rewards, not your individual efforts.

> No matter at what position or situation you are in now, there is always room for improvement.

When attempting to do something different for your team, never ever bring the attitude — 'this is not how I use to do things'. Change that attitude and try and see how the team wants that particular job to be carried out. If you are confident that your idea can bring in better results explain it to other team members unagitatedly. Hear what they have to say and then express your ideas. If your team still sticks to their agenda, support them wholeheartedly and give in your best. What you generally see is that if a person's idea is discouraged or dismissed then they do not participate actively as a part of the team. Or more damaging is the time when the team faces a setback and the person whose idea was earlier shot down, now carries out a tirade because their suggestion was not accepted and that is why the venture failed. Never ever do that but help the team come out of the situation by working along with other members of the team.

"A silent member will never contribute to the team but can only damage the situation even more. Keep your ego aside and go with what the team has decided and work on it to make it a success. That is the true attitude of a team player and by participating wholeheartedly, even though your idea has been rebuked, you display the true spirit of a serving mentality. This attitude of serving will bring in rich dividends as you stand out of the general crowd and get noticed. In the event of changes in the organisation, you are bound to be picked up to move on. The positive energy and vibrations you would display in such a situation are enormous and it also rubs on the entire team and helps the team to perform at its best.

Change or else you will be changed:

Change and adapt to your new team as soon as possible, else the team will change you and look for someone who would change and adapt to the needs of the team. We discard many useless things in our lives, then why wouldn't a team discard its members who are a hindrance to its future growth.

There are organisations which have lost their number one position in the market because they did not change on time. Noticeably, a film manufacturing company which had a huge market share did not change to digital technology on time. Today, seldom does one use films for capturing moments when they have an instant technology available, where they can click pictures and share it with anyone in the world in a fraction of a second. The company lost out on its market share because the manner in which people had now begun taking pictures, sharing and storing them had changed drastically.

Change and Adapt

Large stores with huge investments had to go online to cater to a new breed of online shoppers. Stores which did not change to add this feature, lost out to those who saw the new opportunity coming and set up customer friendly online stores.

We not only have to change but also change for good to be the most useful person in a team. Then only can the team achieve its goal and only then can we achieve our goals too.

Raj sipped the last drop of his *chai* and glanced at his watch. It was almost 4.30 in the evening and I knew the day's wisdom sharing had come to an end. I would now have to wait till next Tuesday for more nuggets of his vast experience. I still could not contain my anxiety and asked him politely, "Raj, so will you be talking about how you excelled in your job as a chef in the new restaurant?"

"Yes, but more about how I prepared myself for the next bigger opportunity that was knocking at my door. So how about meeting again next week same time?"

I said good bye to him. I was glad he had shared some more of his experience and wisdom. And I was really excited at the prospect of meeting him again. Such was his charm.

How to change and adapt:

- Express gratitude: To God, your parents and your guru.
- Change your appearance: Grooming, presentation and positive body language.
- Be more committed: Commit to time, to your work, to your team, to your organisation; commit to yourself.
- Believe in yourself.
- Change your workplace into a vibrant one with a positive atmosphere.
- Be passionate with your work.
- Learn to like things that you dislike.
- Dare to face new challenges.

Points to ponder:
- How do you react to change? Are you threatened or do you accept it as another challenge that you have to overcome?
- Do you accept change as a part of life?
- Do you blame your personal limitations to face changes?

1. _____
2. _____
3. _____

My strengths:

1. _____
2. _____
3. _____

I want to improve:

1. _____
2. _____
3. _____
4. _____

A gem is not polished without rubbing
Nor a man perfected without trials
- Anonymous

Chapter 3

> *Take up one idea. Make that one idea your life — think of it, dream of it, live on that idea. Let the brain, muscles, nerves, every part of your body, be full of that idea, and just leave every other idea alone. This is the way to success; that is the way great spiritual giants are produced.*
>
> **- Swami Vivekananda**
>
> *At least with me, the match starts much, much earlier than the actual match.*
>
> **- Sachin Tendulkar**
>
> *Luck is what happens when preparation meets opportunity.*
>
> **- Seneca**

Importance of Preparation

As always Raj was in his office waiting for me with that effervescent smile. I had been meeting Raj for the past two weeks and his charisma had started influencing me as well. I started smiling genuinely at people and began working on personal issues that earlier I had dreaded to think of changing. I started looking at life more positively and meaningfully. It dawned on me suddenly that Raj has started touching my life too and in this deal I was the sole beneficiary.

As we settled down on the couch, I smiled back at Raj and asked him,

"Last week you shared with me that you started preparing yourself for the next big thing. Do you mind sharing in detail as to what was that and how did you prepare yourself."

Raj settled on the couch and started talking to me.

"The new restaurant started doing well. It got comfortable for me to dream and visualise about a bigger future. One needs to know where they are going and why they are going. It is important to get that clear in the mind; crystallise your thinking about your goal in life. Then the journey of life is more meaningful and enjoyable."

"Once we positioned ourselves in the line of growth it was clear that the rest would fall in place. All we needed to do was to keep moving forward. Positioning is important and once you figure that out, the rest of the journey, though tough, is enjoyable. Position yourself towards your goal, stay focused and move in that direction. No matter what, one day you are bound to reach your goal."

Importance of Preparation

"Assume yourself going to New York from Washington DC. Let us also assume that the only way to reach to New York by road is through Interstate 95 North. Once you are on 'I 95 North' and position yourself towards New York, no matter how slow you travel you are bound to reach New York one day."

"As you start your journey you will not see the 'New York' signboard anywhere; what you will see is the name of the next bigger city that is approaching. Since you are starting from Washington DC you will see Baltimore on the signboard. When you approach Baltimore you will see the sign of Delaware and further down Newark. When you are near Newark only then will you see the sign of New York. Even then you will have to drive over 70 miles to reach New York. If you are not on 'I 95' and not positioned towards New York no matter how fast you travel you will never ever reach New York."

"What we learn from this are two things. First, that positioning yourself in the line of your goal is vital and second, that your ultimate destination is not visible to you at the time you begin your journey."

"We had lived in New York for some time and would pass by this construction site where a huge skyscraper was being built. As we crossed the place on a daily basis, we were able to observe the time that the engineering team spent during the foundation work. We saw how meticulously it was being planned and carried out, and the time taken to lay the foundation. However, once the structure reached the ground floor level, then the rise of the rest of the floors were pretty fast. During the same time there was a 3-storied structure being constructed inside our residential complex.

> **Position yourself towards your goal, stay focused and move in that direction. One day you are bound to reach your goal!**

The foundation work of this building did not take as long as compared to the time taken to lay the foundation of the gigantic tower that was coming up in New York. This taught me an important lesson in life. If you plan to grow big then you need to lay a strong foundation for yourself too. If you ignore that then chances are that it may fall like a pack of cards. We have seen this happening to many people. But the irony is that they blame fate, destiny and everything else but themselves. If only they had realised in advance that they had to first lay a strong foundation before they could climb their ladder to success; then they would not have fallen. And that is why we give so much importance to preparation."

"As mentioned earlier knowing where you are going and why you are going is important in one's life. As the restaurant business progressed, it was decided by then that I wanted to be in the restaurant business. So, I started experimenting by trial and error with the taste buds of our regular clients who frequented the restaurant."

"How did you do that?" I asked him.

"First, by keeping a watch on the finished plates that would come back into the wash area. If the plate was empty or if there was enough leftover on the plates, it gave an idea of what customers liked or disliked. Second, by getting continuous feedbacks from the clients through the boys in the dining area. These two inputs are quite valuable for a restaurateur. Being located in a cosmopolitan area, we had people from different ethnic backgrounds visiting us. A good majority of them were American nationals visiting us with their families, though it was an Indian restaurant. They loved our *dosa* and Indian curries. Our Sunday afternoon buffet was also a huge hit with them."

"The work wasn't easy; later, after spending about a few months into the job, managing the floor

> One person with belief in your team is equivalent to a hundred with just interest in your opposing team.

was also added to my schedule of work. Our own manager too was shuttling between other businesses which were a part of our owner's. My additional charge was challenging, as managing the kitchen itself was a major task and to take additional charge of the floor was backbreaking. The best step possible was to train the guys on the floor and delegate work to them, hundred percent. It was then time for me to learn some people management skills."

"There's an incident that comes to mind, where things actually changed for the better. There was this guest who used to visit our restaurant every day except on Sundays. He always ordered coffee and light snacks and his bill was never over five bucks a day, and he left tips once in a while only. Our floor guys started making fun of him behind his back and at times accidently the message would spill over to other patrons. In spite of not getting a good service, this person continued visiting and enjoyed his coffee and light snacks."

"It could have been possible that ours was the only restaurant between his office block and his residence. Otherwise why would one want to visit a place that gave him poor service?"

"When not busy in the kitchen I would remove my apron and cap and would stand near the cash register. It was a good spot to get a bird's-eye view of the entire dining area from there. The floor staff used to take potshots at this guest but I never realised the seriousness of it until I personally witnessed it one day. They would ignore this 'coffee guest' and would concentrate on patrons whose orders were larger. When this incident was witnessed, they were concentrating more on a client who was not even a regular to our restaurant."

"Next day during lunch break along with my assistant Tony, we called up a meeting and requested for the bill of the coffee guy and the other guest whose bill was closer to seventy bucks. We made the staff do a simple calculation."

"We asked the group as to how many days this 'coffee guy' visited our restaurant and they all said in unison, 'every day except Sundays'. As they said this they all smiled sarcastically. Then raising the seventy bucks bill they were asked as to how many days that guest visited us. They replied that he only came in once a while. When asked if that client visited at least once in a month their reply was a 'no'. Upon request one of the floor assistants multiplied 70 times 12, that is assuming our friend visited us every month and spent $70 at our restaurant. The floor guy said that it came to $840 a year. Then he was asked to multiply 5 times 25 times 12, ($5 x 25 days in a month x 12 months). The floor assistant gave us the figure of $1500. The group was then asked as to who was contributing more towards their salary by bringing more business to us. None of them replied, neither did anyone of them look at us."

"It was quite evident to them now that even if a client spends only five dollars at a time but does it at regular intervals, then that client is contributing more to the business than a client who spends a larger amount and then disappears."

"The meeting ended with a decision that irrespective of what a person is spending at our restaurant, everyone should be treated well and equal. The floor captain was instructed to make sure that this was implemented. After this incident the service was a treat for our customers. We started getting compliments not just for the food but for our services too. Slowly but surely a culture was developing, an identity of our own."

"The staff is good in networking and all of them had only good to talk about our working style. This message went far and across and we started getting quality applications for various posts in the restaurant. Few known investors in the area, when they came to dine, also stopped and started meeting me regularly and the network started expanding slowly."

"That was fantastic Raj; I complimented him."

Develop a burning desire:

> Prevention is better than cure. Preparation is better than repair.

"The success of any person begins with a simple aspiration to achieve something in life. As that simple aspiration gets more intense and a positive instinct develops, it becomes a burning desire. Once we develop that burning desire to succeed, and if we can keep that fuel burning inside us, we will figure out a way to succeed."

Believe in yourself:

"Once we develop that burning desire the first and foremost thing to do is to believe in ourselves. It is vital that we believe in ourselves and believe in our capabilities for others cannot fathom our strengths and weaknesses. One person with belief in your team is equivalent to a hundred with just an interest in your opposing team. If we believe in ourselves then others will be in a better position to help us or guide us to success. Once we display our burning desire along with our belief in ourselves, then we are bound to go places by becoming a good team player."

"I agree with you Raj; a burning desire with a self-belief is an awesome combination. What else did you do as part of preparation," I queried further.

"We realised that if we did not prepare ourselves, then we would end up paying dearly in repair. Prevention is always better than cure .You drive, right? Can you afford a breakdown in the middle of nowhere or on a dead night? All of us take extra care in the maintenance of our vehicles. We make sure that the engine oil is changed on time, the tyre pressure is right, the engine coolant level is perfect, brake oil, transmission fluid — meaning our vehicle is serviced periodically. We are so concerned about every minute detail about the vehicle that we drive; but, what maintenance do we do of the owner of the vehicle. If we don't prepare we end up repairing. And repair is always an expensive affair."

"Take for instance the preparation this magnificent country has gone through after 9/11. Not a single bullet has been allowed to be fired against this country on its soil. Every important location was secured and protected. Every security agency was upgraded and trained for prevention and better warfare. Every citizen prepared themselves as never before. Unfortunately, look at what happened in Mumbai, India on 11/26. Apart from the precious and invaluable lives, some agencies unofficially put the damage closer to Rs. 50,000 crores (about $11 billion) in a 62-hour siege of the city by terrorists. However, if the concerned authorities had invested a fraction of this amount in prevention, don't you think this could have been avoided, especially in view of the country being attacked from all sides for centuries? Yes, indeed it is a matter of pride that the country is up and running again in no time. The spirit of India and its people have to be commended. But for a moment just imagine, if they had succeeded in preventing all these attacks, the growth of the country could have been faster compared to what it is today."

Raj sighed and was silent for some time and then he continued.

"Look at a boxing champion. Ever thought how much time they spend in preparation or training? Their match normally lasts 45 minutes or so. We have even seen a match where Mike Tyson floored his opponent in 3 seconds. You blinked and the match was over. How long do they train or prepare themselves for these magnificent performances?

"May be a year or two." I said.

"Much more, it will not be wrong to say that their preparation starts from the day they decide to become a champion. This could be two years as you said or eight years or may be when they were as young as 6 years old. They start preparing for that one day where they will be in the ring to win as a champion from the moment they decide to become a champion."

Importance of Preparation

"Take for instance a 100-metre sprinter in Olympics which is held every four years. As of today the world record is somewhere near 9.7 seconds. The champions Usain Bolt or Asafa Powell practice every day not just for four years but much in advance. Think of this: for ten seconds of performance they train and prepare six to eight hours on a daily basis for more than four to eight years. And for those of us who have to perform for over forty years at work, how much preparation will be just enough?"

> Healthy body fosters healthy mind. A healthy mind can conquer almost anything.

"Remember we used to do it while we were in schools. We used to learn and do homework throughout the year to sit for that final exam at the end of the academic year. But when we grew up and got a job based on the preparation that we did till that day, we gave up and almost swore never to learn again. We forgot about that basic foundation that we ourselves built and which brought us so far in life. It is very wisely said that what we are today is the result of the sum of the preparation we did till yesterday. What we will be tomorrow will solely be based on the preparation we do now. If you have ignored the preparation part and gone into a lazy mode, then this is the time to get out of your comfort zone; if not, the future will soon turn uncomfortable for you."

"Do you remember the fable about the dog who was sitting on a nail, moaning but lazy enough to get up and move. Seeing this, a young disciple asked the saint, "*Guru ji* why is the dog refusing to get up and move." The guru replies, "because the pain is not painful enough to the dog."

Invest in your health:

"Every spiritual guru and every motivational speaker talks about conquering the mind. If you conquer your mind you can make your mind your best friend else it will be your worst enemy and you are bound to be its slave. A healthy body fosters a healthy mind."

"I neglected the most precious gift god had given me — my health — by eating junk food and not sticking to an eating schedule. Fast food especially deep fried food, sodas and beer were common in my diet; either all of them together or one after the other. My health soon went for a toss. My energy levels started dipping and my weight started increasing. Fortunately we had a client, a nutritionist, who would visit us once in a while; she would always order low-calorie but rich nutritious food. She would request for a mix-match and we were willing to try it out. We were getting free recipes." Raj winked and continued.

"After consulting the nutritionist and after understanding my eating and drinking habits she prescribed a few tests and asked me to see her with the results. Well you know what happened when the results came in. She asked if she could be blunt or if I wanted her to be diplomatic. I said that she was free to express herself the way she felt it was right. Then she dropped the bombshell; she said that I was dying a slow death, which was due to the junk that I was eating. She recommended a complete shift in my diet by asking me to change my eating, drinking and sleeping habit. She also packed me off to a gym. It took me about six months to make a complete shift from unhealthy foods to eating quality healthy food. It was like getting back to 'eating to live' from 'living to eat'."

We both had a good laugh at the humour and Raj continued.

"The new healthy food habit gave a new lease of life. My energy was not just back but now my stamina had also improved. During the days of consuming junk, it was difficult to go for a brisk walk for even 10 steps but now a good forty five minutes run on the treadmill was easy. Even my skin had a dead look those days."

I interrupted, "it is glowing now. What exactly did you change in your food habit?"

He thanked me for the compliment and continued.

"I simply stuck to the diet I was suggested and most importantly I took the quantity of food my nutritionist advised me to take. She informed me that seventy percent of our planet is water so is our body, therefore it is wise to have food that contains seventy percent water. Mostly, freshly cut vegetable salads, a well-balanced diet and good amounts of fresh fruits in between. I was asked to avoid eating all kinds of red meat, and taking vitamin supplements was something new to me."

"We spend a good amount in polishing our car so that it shines. Don't you think we should at least spend a fraction of that amount on a good skin moisturiser? My logic is simple; I feel the owner should outshine the car he drives."

"All these changes were a tedious task and definitely did not come easy. Success is a choice and after having chosen to go for it, we should not compromise on anything — we have to give it our best. I didn't want my health to pose challenges and create obstacles on my way to success."

> What we are today is the result on the sum of the preparation we did till yesterday. What we will be tomorrow will solely be based on the preparation we do now.

Develop a magnetic personality:

"I could not help but notice that when certain people entered the restaurant there was an instant uplifting sense all around. Even while inside the kitchen I could sense these positive vibrations and I would come out and meet these people walking into the restaurant. These people had a certain pull on the people around them and one developed an instant liking for them. I started observing and studying them. They were always well groomed, dressed neatly and walked confidently. They were calm, collected and even spoke to our staff very politely. Since all types of people visited the restaurant, it was a good observation point for studying human behaviour. I made sure that this advantage was utilised to the fullest. This observation helped bring in some positive changes in my dressing sense and grooming, and I was learning to be humble too."

"During my initial days of achieving some success, I was extremely arrogant and self-centered. My early success did go to my head and I behaved snobbishly many times, which was quite damaging. After losing a lot of good friends, I began to make new contacts and develop friendships, and also had to learn how to keep them. I still carry regrets of losing some extremely good friends; even though I apologized to them, I could not regain their friendship."

Widen contacts:

"Being an introvert, I only interacted with people who approached me or those who were introduced to me by my existing contacts. But now I had to break that shackle and extend my hand to strangers and say hello with a smile. It was a struggle, initially, to work towards developing and maintaining good ethical relationships. The stumbling block was the low self-image. Changing the dressing style was one way to improve my self-image and the next step now was to work on my self-confidence. At the same time I went about improving what I was not good at, constantly striving to be a shade better than yesterday. With the new-gained confidence and a better self-image, I went about expanding my contacts locally and globally too."

"When you have a wide network of friends and contacts it is like an all-weather protection as well as an image booster. It is amazing to see how even a herculean task look miniscule, when you use your network to help solve the issues or get a control over situations."

Learn to manage funds:

"I was a spendthrift and always ended up spending more than I earned. It was insanity; I used credit cards senselessly, flaunting a dozen cards and generously treating friends on borrowed money. Buying stuffs which I probably did not even deserve on credit was considered cool. If I had to pay cash for those items, I seriously doubt if I would have actually even picked them up. It was quite a revelation to see how some guys would spend less while paying cash and more if they swiped a card. I was foolishly pampering myself with money which wasn't there in the first place, and later I had to work through many years to pay that off. I put a break on all unnecessary spending and slowly repaid the credit card debt and later had them cancelled one by one. I just kept a single card to be used to boost my credit ratings. Over a period of time, I started putting away ten percent of the income into a saving account. Savings soon became a priority, and I started living on the rest of the money. A decision was taken to live and meet all expenses with the remaining ninety percent. By just reversing my priorities the much dented confidence started shaping up well."

Anger Management:

"This was one habit I had a tough time reining in. I was extremely egoistic, arrogant and hot headed. It was easy for me to blame the old baggage and past hurt feelings and say it was ventilation time. But that was definitely not right. It not only hurt me but brought in irreparable loss in relationships. The end result was that I was already carrying enough damaged luggage and I was adding on to it further. It was weighing on me big time and pulling me back in every endeavour I indulged in. My counsellor guided me to forget and forgive. This was again not easy for me but I was determined to succeed."

"My counsellor told me that if I focused on the past I would never be able to make a future. Instead, he showed me how to catch myself thinking about the negative past and then to try and focus on a bright future and force my mind away from the past. I also began meditating and exercising using the deep breathing method and started associating myself more with cheerful people. It was a long process but by keeping on it I was able to control my temper to a larger extent. Earlier I would explode instantly at the sight of a mistake or something unpleasant. But after going through the counselling sessions, I started delaying my response time and slowly started looking at alternative solutions. This helped me gain better control on my rage issue. Now, I would give some time to think about it, weight the pros and cons, then would discuss it out rather than resorting to an instant shouting match. Slowly but steadily I overcame my anger."

Ego and humility:

"Ego was another major problem with me. My sudden success went straight to my head. When my income went to $2500 from a mere $800 along with my change in designation, all this made me very egotistic. Earlier I was an average person but the sudden transition changed me in a negative way. I started ill-treating people and developed that 'I know everything' attitude. It took me some time to realise that people actually started staying away from me or came to me only if they could not avoid me. As I was open to suggestions an old well wisher sat me down and advised me on the goodness of being humble. To understand this he asked me to observe the people who walked into the restaurant, and I instantly saw that the successful people were the most humble."

"Another thing which he told me was that it was good to love the self but the charm is when you love others. I was too blind to look at the nice people around me, my colleagues, friends, guests, vendors, etc. He taught me to start greeting these people with a smile and let it slowly grow. I had to develop this habit as people usually stay away from egoistic and adamant guys. He also said that I was too self-centered and it was all about 'me and mine'. I needed to let go of that feeling and focus on others, their likes, dislikes and growth. We cannot grow without the support of people around us. One other lesson he taught me was that the more successful I become the more humble I should try to be. He gave me a simple remedy. He asked me to speak less of my achievements and talk more about the other person's work or their accomplishments."

"I am doing just the opposite now, right?" Raj asked me quizzically.

"Oh no Raj, how will you otherwise answer my questions which are directly related to you and your actions and reactions," I responded.

Raj then continued from where he had stopped.

Improve and prove your integrity:

"I was atrocious when it came to returning borrowed money. I mentioned earlier how I would spend more than my income. I borrowed from friends, relatives and banks. Banks were ever ready to lend me more. They were a happy lot because I was happy paying the required minimum amount of five percent. My tax consultant was a nice person; he helped me to get out of that vicious circle. After I cleared all my debts, I was a free man and breathed easily. My smile was genuine and I didn't have to act anymore."

"Most business operation required that loans be taken for various things and as the business expanded, the requirement of loans also was more. However, we made it a point to return the borrowed funds on or before the due date. This helped tremendously to build trustworthiness. The lenders developed a safe zone in us. Once we proved our genuineness and our integrity, money was never a problem for our ventures. They would come to us and offer funds, and promised us that even half a million was just a phone call away. Honestly, there was a time when a mere five hundred bucks help from someone would be life saving to me. Let me confess that the debt-free status boosted my confidence and self-image."

Weed out negative thinking:

"Negativity was inbuilt in me. I would only look at the negatives and would ignore the positives around me. My focus was always on the wrong side. For instance, I would look at the dirt around a plant and think about it and totally ignore the beautiful flowers on the plant. Needless to say I did miss some beautiful rainbows in my life. Working on my attitude and attempting to be positive all the time was a conscious move. Moving out of the gossiping and inactive group and staying with people who had a progressive mind helped deal with this trait."

"Earlier I would open my eyes to the newspaper in the morning followed by my cup of coffee. That changed to staying put in bed for a few extra seconds and offering gratitude to God for gifting me another beautiful day to live. I would then briefly visualise the good things that could be accomplished on that day. I mentally made a list of people who could be associated positively with that day. After refreshing myself I would meditate for a few minutes and then pray. Over a short period of time I was able to do away with negative thinking or let negativity influence me in any way. I learned how to skillfully keep negative people at a distance and I never gave them a chance to feel that I was doing that deliberately. I had to work hard in figuring out a way to keep emotional blackmailers at bay without hurting our relationship. All they did was drain me of my energy and make me weak in the knees. I worked extra to surround myself with positive-thinking people and achievers."

Learn to like things that need to be done:

"Any kind of job which helped the team and the organisation was done with utmost sincerity irrespective of whether I liked that particular work or job. By doing what is necessary first and then tackling what is generally possible by a person, most of us can do what we think as impossible. The easiest way to do an unpleasant job is to develop a liking towards it. Once that is in place every job can be taken care of."

Learn to follow instructions:

"Generally it is impossible for people to follow instructions to the 'T'. Free your mind from the cluster of bad thoughts and let new information and good thoughts flow in. Follow instructions from your seniors or your clients. Our job is to satisfy their requirement; this does not mean you shouldn't voice your thoughts or suggestions. Even after hearing your suggestions, if they insist on that they want the job done the way they had explained earlier then do it exactly the way it has been explained to you. When it comes to instructions, priority should always be given to the person we report to. Their satisfaction should be our motto."

Start and end the day with positive thoughts:

"As I said earlier, I forced myself to change the way I began my morning. If we read or listen to something positive in the morning it generally sets a positive trend for the day ahead. The positive mood developed during the beginning of the day itself gives us the energy to fight the negativities throughout the day. End the day with something positive, either by reading or listening to soothing music or anything that relaxes you. This will help us program the subconscious mind to more positives. The subconscious mind is active while we sleep and if we constantly feed positives to it then it starts giving us back the positive defense system when we are awake."

Learn to give and give it right:

"I was never a giver. It would have been better to call me a receiver, whether it was gifts or help from someone. We see that majority of the people enjoy receiving. But if we want to receive in abundance then we need to start giving too. I started reading about philanthropy and how to give, how much to give and where to give. We are enjoying this life because of God. He is the owner of everything and I had to pay the rent for living in his beautiful kingdom. A small amount of money from the pay check was kept aside every month towards charity. At the end of the year this would add up to make a decent amount. Sponsoring young and bright needy kids and paying for their school fees was a good way to start."

"It was carried out anonymously by sending the fees directly to the school and requesting them not to divulge any information about the sponsor. As our business grew, the ten percent amount also grew every year, and we were able to donate to charities which managed these activities more professionally."

"One thing that we learned during philanthropy was that if the money we donated was not utilised in a noble way by the charities or the receiver it could dent our blessings. So I did my own research and always tried to give it to the right people who helped the needy in the right way without any hidden motives. In the beginning the donation was a meager amount but as the donation amount increased every year my own income grew multi-fold."

"Raj is it okay to ask how much you donated last year?" I asked anxiously.

"Sure, why not. Last year we were able to donate more than $200,000." Raj replied and then continued.

Sharpen your axe:

Abraham Lincoln once said that if he had to chop a tree in six hours then he would spend four hours sharpening his axe. All successful people realise the importance of preparation, individually as well as collectively. Having realised what you are preparing for, make a list of logistics and skills required to tackle the challenge. Once you identify your weakness, work to improve upon them and become strong in the area of your weakness.

"In short I was making myself a better person so that I became the biggest asset to my team."

I was so engrossed at the fantastic wisdom nuggets Raj shared that it was only when he looked at the watch that we both realised that it was past 6 pm. I was apologetic for keeping him so long but then Raj pacified me saying that he was also relaxed since he did not have any appointments that evening. He said that may be due to his mind being relaxed it did not warn him of the 4.30 pm cut off time.

We both had a good laugh and I thanked him for the wonderful life-changing pointers that he had just shared with me. We agreed to meet up again next Tuesday and I left his office.

How do you prepare:

- Study and understand the project
- Have a clear understanding of your role in the project
- Write down the list of man, machine and skills required to achieve your target
- Decide a genuine time frame to achieve your target
- Analyze your strengths and weaknesses
- Accept your weaknesses and work to improve upon them until you are able to overcome them
- Observe and learn from members of other stronger teams
- Try and learn how you can assist your teammate to perform better

Points to ponder:

- Do you underestimate preparation?
- How do you rate yourself when it comes to preparing?
- Do you go that extra mile in overcoming hesitations to prepare?
- How do you overcome procrastination?

1. _____

2. _____

3. _____

My strengths:

1. _____

2. _____

3. _____

4. _____

I want to improve:

1. _____

2. _____

3. _____

4. _____

> *By failing to prepare you are preparing to fail.*
>
> **- Benjamin Franklin**

Chapter 4

Therefore all things whatsoever ye would that men should do to you, do ye even so to them.

— **Matthew 7:12**

Sometimes one creates a dynamic impression by saying something, and sometimes one creates as significant an impression by remaining silent.

— **Dalai Lama**

I am a success today because I had a friend who believed in me and I didn't have the heart to let him down...

— **Abraham Lincoln**

Communicate to Develop Relationships

Raj greeted me as usual in his spacious office and after settling down we went over, briefly, on what we had discussed the previous week.

Raj ordered for tea for both of us through the intercom and then continued from where we had stopped last week.

"After the recently concluded soccer world cup, Andreas Iniesta, Spain's goal scoring hero in the final, confessed that the team won because the team stuck to the philosophy of passing and communicating to each other constantly."

"Two people need to team up for our birth and double that after our death. There cannot be a better indicator than this that TEAMWORK is an important skill we need to master during our life time."

"Communication has become a vital tool in not just developing relations but maintaining it as well. If you have one more person working with you then you have a team. The only way you communicate with your team member is through interaction. Those interactions need to be positive to develop a relationship. A relationship is developed when you trust your partner or your teammate. To build trust you need to build confidence in them and that is possible only through positive interactions. This is where communication becomes so vital. To begin with we can learn a lot from nature itself."

Communicate to Develop Relationships

"Nature is our best teacher. It teaches us a lot, but we are so engrossed in our day-to-day mundane work that either we do not see it at all or even if we do see it then we do not understand it one bit. After having decided to keep an open mind, I was able to see and understand a lot of stuff that we actually see around us on a day-to-day basis. After I changed my life style I started going for walks in parks and enjoyed the lake side."

> Two people need to team up for our birth and double that after our death. There cannot be a better indicator than this that TEAMWORK is an important skill we need to master during our life time.

"On one such day when I was taking a walk along the Potomac River near Jefferson memorial, I saw a flock of birds flying in a V formation. As they went past above me, I noticed that the bird which was leading the flock had moved all the way back, and the bird which was right behind the leading bird had now taken the leading position. I looked at them till they disappeared from my view. Till then neither had I noticed such a phenomenon nor had I read about it anywhere. I wondered how they planned, communicated and then executed this to perfection. I could see a clear execution of communication, selfless commitment to the cause, collaboration and a sense of mission in their actions. When I returned, I mentioned this event to a few of my intelligent and well-read friends. They said they knew about this since their childhood."

"They said that the birds I saw were geese and they flew in this formation to cover greater distances which individually they may not be able to cover. By flying in a V formation the whole flock added up to seventy one percent greater flying range than if each flew alone. At that point I thought, 'wow' that's amazing, and why can't we incorporate that in our lives. Here another friend interrupted us and said that this was now being taught in almost every organisation during their team building and training sessions."

"My friend stays near a brook overlooking a wooded area. I always spend some time on their patio enjoying the beautiful view from there. On one such visit while enjoying the view I noticed a bunch of big ants forming a cluster to cross over from one tree branch to another branch. The ant was not even a centimetre long and the gap between the two branches was about five or six centimetres. The ants grouped themselves together into a ball and then extended this formation to the next branch and instantly all of them had managed to cross over. I started wondering how on earth these tiny ants communicated among themselves before, during and after the task. From the first ant which held on to this side of the trunk to the last ant which crossed over after they formed into a ball, how might they have communicated one way or another about their intention. As I sat there looking amazingly at the event unfolding in front of me, I remembered a story which I had read in primary school. It was about a big fish that used to attack the habitat of small fishes and eat them up. Worried about losing their entire flock, one day a smart tiny fish struck up on the idea that next time when the big fish came to attack them the entire school of small fish would form into the shape of a much bigger fish and thus defend themselves. As planned, the next time when the big fish came to attack the small fishes' colony it saw a gigantic fish swimming menacingly towards it. The story goes that the big fish was terrified by the giant fish coming to swallow it and never came to attack the smaller fishes again."

"I sat there in bewilderment in the new realisation that how much a TEAM and communication within the team is important to all of us. Also, how nature has been revealing to us the importance of a team. It is absolutely true that **T**ogether **E**veryone **A**chieves **M**iracles. And as we grow up to adults we forget all the important lessons of life. In all the three events mentioned earlier on land, sea and air every member of the team acted with total commitment and loyalty. Not a single one of them ignored the duty assigned to them. They were submissive to the mission. Even if there was someone who objected to the whole idea, each member of the team went ahead and gave it their best once a decision was arrived at and then acted upon it. Armed with this new experience and information, I vowed to be a good team player and to communicate efficiently and effectively to inspire others to work as a team. I realized the futility of working alone and the immense benefit one derives by working as a team."

Be the ice breaker:

Most people are hesitant to start a conversation. It's simple. It all starts with just a smile and then a hello. Be the first person to smile, and the only way you can get a stranger to smile at you is by smiling at them the moment your eyes meet. If you delay

> A team gels through communication and bonds through relationships.

then the delay is permanent. Do not wait endlessly with team members to begin a dialogue. Be the initiator. While communicating with others ask nonthreatening questions. This will put them at ease and they will open up to a healthy dialogue. When two people share each other's views and when they find that they have a lot in common is when a relationship begins.

Compliment others:

"The best way to develop a relationship is by giving sincere compliments to others. We perform to our optimum when we are complimented. However, if you ask people as to when was the last time they got complimented, very few are able to recollect, while some of them even surprisingly say that they have never received any compliments. Does that mean if they received compliments they would have performed better? Research indicates that they would have."

"We perform better when we are inspired, and we get inspiration from someone complimenting us. In the absence of anyone complimenting us how do we get inspired? Quite simple, just compliment others. When we compliment others they feel good and that good feeling transmits back to us thereby inspiring and motivating us. Do not wait for others to compliment you so that you can perform to your optimum level. Shift the focus from you and focus on others."

"Spend some time, probe and find out something good your teammates have done and compliment them. If you do this constantly your own performance will get a boost and you will easily develop a good and long-lasting relationship with your team and others."

Become an active listener:

"We have been bestowed with two ears and a single mouth. That itself shows that we need to listen twice as much as we speak. People are fond of those who listen to them. Instead of merely listening become an active listener. Ask open-ended questions that would encourage them to talk to you. An active listener encourages the person to share more; by doing so they share their experiences and develop a liking for each other. This helps in building relationships."

"When talking to your teams first listen to your team members. Give them a chance to share and express their ideas. Understand what they have to share which will boost the performance of the team. Merely by becoming a good listener you can get into the good books of people."

Use plural instead of singular:

"Once you learn how to make others open up to you an important factor to be practiced is to start using plural while talking to them. Always use 'we', 'us' or 'our' instead of 'I', 'me' or 'mine'. This will show that you are not taking any individual credit for the team's accomplishments. Your teammates will be happy and will perform better when they are given credit for their hard work. However, if you take credit for their hard work, which might happen when you say 'I' instead of 'we' then the team performance might take a beating. So to boost a team's performance always use plural instead of singular while communicating with others."

Reach a consensus:

"Incorporate ideas put forward by the team which will benefit the team and the organisation as a whole. Include every member of your team during discussions. Be open and discuss issues threadbare. Do not hide any facts that would endanger the mission later on. After ironing out the differences, reach a consensus by discussion. All discussions have to be done in a sober way and never in an agitated manner otherwise this may damage the atmosphere of communication. It is often possible that sometimes during brainstorming a team member would put forward an idea that might be absurd. Care has to be taken that they should not be ridiculed or insulted. Try not to disagree with your team members outright. People dislike those who oppose them; instead, skillfully agree to their points but explain to them why sticking to the team's decision will be more fruitful to each member of the team. Always be in control of the discussion and steer it always to a point of decision that benefits the team.

Think win-win-win:

"At any point of time your action should always be to reach a win-win-win situation. Which simply means that the organisation you work for should benefit from the action you are about to take, your team should benefit and finally you should benefit. If any party in the deal loses then it is a loss for everyone. If your team or organisation loses and you win it will not last long. It is a temporary success and eventually you stand to lose big."

Make SMART Decisions

You	Your Team	Your Organisation	Result
Win	lose	lose	-ve
Win	win	lose	-ve
Lose	win	win	-ve
Lose	lose	win	-ve
Lose	lose	lose	-ve
Win	win	win	+ve

In the above illustration it is apparent that any other position other than a win for all the parties involved is a losing proposition. If any of the party is losing then no one is gaining either.

Express and Explain Expectations:

"Inform and be informed. That is as simple as it can get. Inform in detail to your team about the entire project in minute details. Do not withhold any information from the team. Likewise, make sure you are kept informed about all the activities of the team pertaining to the project you are handling."

"Start your day with a short meeting with your team. Touch upon what the team wants to accomplish that day. Encourage everyone to do their best and express your expectations from them. If you have a slogan or prayer, say it together to build the synergy of the team."

"We had a poster with a smiley along with our mission statement 'serving with a smile' on the door which leads to the dining area. Any person going to the dining area from the kitchen

> The only way you can get a stranger to smile at you is by smiling at them the moment you lock eyes. If you delay then the delay is permanent.

fixes their attitude to positive while entering the dining area. Similarly we decided that we would leave all our personal issues at the entrance door and never bring the stress into the work area to pass it on to our team members. However, we were all together to tackle any of our team member's issues. This way we ensured that we communicated well with each other and we got together well to solve issues that we could help each other with."

Invest your time:

"You have to take time out and spend time with your team mates. Invest quality time with them and build a longstanding relationship. Most of us spend most of our 'wake-up time' with our team. Let us assume you spend about 14 hours at home or with family, but of those seven hours go towards your sleep. You are left with seven hours of 'wake-up time' with your family provided you are at home or with family for those seven hours of the day. Does it not make sense to be more careful and tender with our relations with our team with whom we spend more 'wake-up time'?"

"Our team helps us to get rewards and we spend most of those rewards on our family. I guess we need to treat our team once in a while who is actually helping us have good family time."

Project your TEAM and never yourself:

A true team player will always project the team in all circumstances. They will always talk good about the team and its achievements to others. A person who promotes themselves over a team can never be a team player. By promoting themselves they will not only isolate themselves from the team but also repel future prospects as well. When a person promotes themselves above a team's achievements, there is always a chance that they will jeopardise the support they have been receiving from other teammates.

Do not isolate yourself:

"Always be approachable. If you build a wall around you, in most likelihood you would yourself be jailed in it. You will suffocate due to lack of information as there is no communication. Mingle with the team, communicate and make yourself approachable to every member of the team. You can steer the team to great success when you know the pulse of the team. If your challenge is bigger, obviously you will need a bigger team to tackle the challenge. The bigger the team the deeper should be the communication."

Connect and stay connected:

"Connect with your team and stay connected. This ensures that no misunderstanding or miscommunication creeps in that would endanger your mission. By not isolating yourself you do give a chance to your team members to reach and communicate with you. But you go a step further and take proactive actions to stay connected with your team. As I said earlier the team leader or captain needs to know the pulse of the team all the time. Be in constant communication and work towards developing and building a relationship with your team members. Once you have a strong and deep-rooted relationship with your team members you can face any challenges."

You can connect with your team using the following tips:
- Talk to impress not to depress or suppress
- Disagree with the team members only in a friendly tone
- Under-promise and over-deliver
- Give credit to your team members for their contribution
- Never criticise your team members in front of others

Be genuine and sincere:

"If you ever have to promise about certain things to your teammate or your client be extremely honest and sincere about it. The best way is to under-promise and over deliver.

Also when you put the effort to develop relationships, talk only about things you are actually serious about. Do not try to impress people with what you do not intend to do. It will have a negative impact contradictory to what you believe would be the outcome."

Communicate to inspire:

"Communication is the greatest tool that you have with you to build a strong-willed team. Choose every opportunity available to boost your team and motivate them. Find reasons to cheer them and cheer them for the smallest achievement on the way to the larger goal. Do not wait till they accomplish the task to cheer your team members. Do it often, be meaningful and realistic. You don't need to give a big lecture or be loud to inspire your team members; you can even give a sincere smile or a thumbs up sign while you pass by them. When praising your team members make sure that you are praising the action and not the person."

"Always give credit to the team where it is due and keep edifying your team while talking to others. The grapevine in your work area should always say that you talk good about the team and that you are always positive about the outcome. One can never achieve anything on their own. There are always people involved in one's own accomplishment. Never ever garner the credit to self; find ways to credit the people involved in your accomplishment."

"Tongue is the sharpest weapon if used improperly. It can slice through the toughest person and can cause irreparable damage. If used wisely it could also be your greatest blessing. Have you not heard people saying, 'Oh! He is a smooth talker'. If you are not one observe and practice."

"At times you may have to reprimand a team member or you may want to show them the right way of doings things. However, criticizing a team member in front of others is a total no-no. Even children do not like to be scolded in front of their siblings."

"If you don't have anything good to tell your team members at least do not share anything that would dampen the team spirit. Many a times staying silent at the right moment is also a boon. In short any attempt at communicating with your team has to be with the single motto of building relationships and bonding for a life time."

How to develop fruitful relationships:

- Master people skills
- Practice becoming an active listener
- Be proactive in building relationships
- Correct your attitude to attract people into your life
- Be humble yet firm
- Under-promise and over deliver.
- Keep your promises
- End disagreements in a friendly way
- Debates may spoil relationships; handle them skillfully

Points to ponder:

- Are you the first one to extend your hand with a smile when meeting a stranger?
- Are people happy to be around you?
- How many genuine friends do you have who will drop everything and come to your assistance in the hour of need?
- How much do you know about the people who are working with you?

1. _____

2. _____

3. _____

My strengths:

1. _____
2. _____
3. _____
4. _____
5. _____

I want to improve:

1. _____
2. _____
3. _____
4. _____
5. _____

> *It is a waste of energy to be angry with a man who behaves badly, just as it is to be angry with a car that won't go.*
> **- Bertrand Russell**

Chapter 5

Thy right is to work only; but never to its fruits;
Not the fruits of action be thy motive.
May you not have any attachment to inaction.
- Bhgavad Gita (Ch2; Text 47)

"When we are debating an issue, loyalty means giving me your honest opinion, whether you think I'll like it or not. Disagreement, at this stage, stimulates me. But once a decision has been made, the debate ends. From that point on, loyalty means executing the decision as if it were your own."
- Colin Powell

"There are plenty of teams in every sport that have great players and never win titles. Most of the time, those players aren't willing to sacrifice for the greater good of the team. The funny thing is, in the end, their unwillingness to sacrifice only makes individual goals more difficult to achieve. One thing I believe to the fullest is that if you think and achieve as a team, the individual accolades will take care of themselves. Talent wins games, but teamwork and intelligence win championships."
- Michael Jordan

Commit with a Selfless Attitude

Raj asked me if I had time. When I said "yes" he then wanted to share with me another success secret he had mastered. He wanted to accommodate since Raj was attending a training program on Advanced Accounting.

I said to myself, "look at this guy so successful but still yearning to learn more."

"Tell me something about your owner — the guy who gave you your first major break," I asked Raj.

"His name was Anand."

"You used his principle to succeed; I am sure he is as successful as you are today. Tell me something about him also."

"Unfortunately Anand died a slow death in business. He always had a purpose behind his idea of helping people. If he had been genuine in his efforts, I am confident he would have been a more successful person today. He was one of the most talented people I had ever seen or heard. You name it and he had that talent. He was also one of the finest chefs I had come across. I learned a valuable lesson through his association that when giving give selflessly. Never expect anything in return for the help you do to other people. You give and move on; find

> When you help others do not expect anything in return. Do it as absolute charity.

more people you can touch positively and then move on. Be on a constant move, helping people achieve in their life by providing whatever you are capable of. When you help someone with a hidden agenda it has a malicious side, an ugly side of exploitation."

"Unfortunately, a few business decisions that Anand took backfired. As Abraham Lincoln once said, 'you cannot fool everyone every time'. Anand's image in the banking circle damaged the situation further. The only way he could salvage the situation was to sell a few of his businesses to restructure himself. That is when Anand told me that he would have to sell the restaurant, which I was managing then. We were doing a lot better compared to the other restaurants in the area. I tried my best to convince him not to sell the unit, but he was adamant. Once Anand decided on something it was next to impossible to reason him out of it, even if it was detrimental to his growth. For me the news of closure was like getting struck by lightning. The news was quite obviously disturbing, and I had a tough time revealing to the team about the troubling time they faced. But being a well-knit team that was connected deeply, I had to prepare the team and tell them of the impending danger that lay ahead of us. Next day during the lunch break they all assembled and said that they will stick with me and be with me wherever I went; and that salary was not a concern. They said that they trusted me and were confident that whatever we would do as a team would flourish. This was not only flattering to me but it also gave me a lot of courage and confidence.

"Then they proposed the unthinkable! They asked me to take over the restaurant and said that they would take any cut in their pay cheque and would stand by me till death does us apart. I was dumbstruck. I had never realised that our bonding was so

> **Even bigger challenges look small when a team with commitment tackles it.**

solid. I could not hold back my emotions and we all hugged and cried. The strength we derived and the synergy that flowed after this incident was something that I will always cherish. The sale price being asked for the restaurant was beyond our financial capacity even when we all tried to pool in the amount."

"Then one of the guys from the staff, AJ (Ajay) said, "Sir, when Anand bought this restaurant he had to take a loan. At that time this place was a mess. Why don't you also approach someone and take a loan. We are doing well and any one will give you a loan."

"It took some time for me to absorb the idea. The next day I approached a businessman client who was our regular patron. We had once rescued him from an embarrassing situation. He was celebrating his son's graduation ceremony and in the nth minute the catering contractor informed him that they would not be able to cater at the event. I still remember how that afternoon he came panting into our place and requested help. We had to decline because we had catered to a party the previous night and the staff had been working throughout the night. As it was a Saturday, I was busy at the restaurant and had not slept a wink till then. If I took his order, then we would be working without sleep for more than thirty-four straight hours. I explained to him our situation and he was almost weeping. I said to him, 'if the staff is ready, we can certainly accommodate you.' Saying this I went to check with the staff to see if they were ready to stretch. They were always a ready lot and I went back to my client at the reception and told him that we were ready to cater to his function. The party went off well and everyone appreciated our contribution."

"As the guest's started leaving and we started packing up, the businessman came and thanked us and said, 'Raj I know you have been working for thirty to forty hours continuously and your enthusiasm and energy baffles me even at this hour. Now that you know my house, if you ever need any help you are welcome to walk in at any time. You guys have saved me from a major embarrassment and disaster.' He said that he would visit the restaurant in the afternoon to settle the bill. When we went to the restaurant the next day, not only had the bill been settled but there was also a cash envelope for all of us!"

"Taking cue from AJ, I phoned our businessman friend and told him that I wanted to meet him to discuss some serious matter. He said he was coming down to the restaurant in the evening and we could discuss the matter then. So that evening after he had his dinner, I told him about our situation and mentioned that the entire staff was with me in this endeavour, and that it was them who had proposed this idea. He spoke to the staff and was extremely happy with their enthusiasm. More than that, he could not think of this place being torn down, because all his friends and family has taken an immense liking to this place and food."

> Ask yourself every day, "How good can I be today?" At the end of the day ask yourself again, "How good have I been today?"

"He said he would finance the project and that I could pay him back within two years or earlier. He further added that he was not into any partnership with me but he would keep all documents with him until I returned the loan. We mutually agreed on an ongoing interest rate. He said he had full confidence in our team and that we would pull this off. He also offered to negotiate the deal on my behalf, because he felt that his experience would help garner a better deal. Further, he confided that it was possible that Anand may not be too keen in selling the restaurant to him and even if he did, he may quote an unreasonable price. I had a fair idea about the offer that Anand was receiving and also the price that he was demanding. Armed with this information, it was easy for my businessman friend to strike a deal even lower than the offer Anand was receiving, because my friend was offering hundred-percent cash down."

"It was a great feeling to own the place where I had once slogged. Life had never been the same after that. I thanked each and every one for bringing all these great souls in my life who positively touched my life one way or the other. Later in one of the gatherings my businessman friend introduced me to his wealthy friends and told them about how I had helped him out once. He narrated how that one incident, of my commitment to work, had made me an entrepreneur."

"My TEAM was always a priority and the TEAM was always there for me. They were a one committed lot and always amazed me with their work ethics. And that is how I ended up owning my own restaurant with the help of a few friends and most importantly my dedicated staff. It was a great feeling to own what I had once built with my team. It was tough initially but fortunately my team stood by me and helped me through the rough weather. At every opportunity I helped them generously in a way I was capable of at that time."

"After we took over the restaurant, the team was even more forthcoming with their ideas and suggested a lot of improvements. Once we implemented some of these suggestions and carried out some modifications in the look of the restaurant and the menu, everything got transformed to a much higher taste. I asked my staff as to why were they so forthcoming with sharing these wonderful ideas with me while they hardly ever suggested anything to Anand when he owned this place. Their reply taught me a big lesson in life. They said that Anand treated them as employees, but I gave them a sense of belonging here. I made them feel as if they owned this place!"

Self-Development:

"Spend time, energy and money in continuous self-development and self-growth lifelong. Keep upgrading your own knowledge and skills and that of your team too. When you keep adding value to yourself there is a retrospective effect on the team. Start your day by asking yourself, 'How good can I be today?' At the end of the day ask yourself again, 'How good have I been today'?"

Submit, not just support:

"When you work with a team it is obvious that you support your team. But teamwork is beyond that; teamwork requires every member to submit to the team even when they disagree. As I had mentioned earlier, at times you may differ with what the team decides but once a decision is arrived at you need to simply abandon your agenda and submit to the team's agenda and work towards making it a success. If you do not actively support your team, then it is nothing but axing the branch that you are sitting on. The team obviously will suffer but your downfall is imminent."

In the soccer world cup final of 2010 (Spain v/s Netherlands) the match was tough and goalless till the final moments of the game. Towards the final 15 minutes or so the Spain forward striker got an excellent chance when he got the ball to himself. He noticed that there were none of Netherland's defenders in sight; moreover another ace striker was in position near the goal, surprisingly unmarked! It was a rare golden moment in the history of soccer and an easy pass would have put the Spanish score to a 1–0 lead, but the striker chose not to pass the ball and toyed with the idea of shooting the ball himself to score the goal. That split second delay was enough for Netherland's defenders to cover him and take the ball away from him. His selfish idea to score the goal by himself denied Spanish a golden goal. Had it not been for Andres Iniesta, the spectacular Spanish striker, who struck the single goal of the match, it could have been a different story had the match been reduced to a shoot out. The selfish player was immediately pulled out by the coach so as not to dampen the spirits of the remaining players. This proved to be a wonderful move, because in the very next few moments Iniesta struck gold, turning a beautiful pass from his colleague into the sole goal of the match.

Forgo your ego:

The dictionary meaning of selflessness means the act of sacrificing one's own interest for the greater good. People project themselves to garner attention; instead ironically it is those who demonstrate selfless attitude, are the ones who garner much attention. It is our false ego that wants to garner credit and attention. If we forgo our pride and surrender our ego, we will be in a better position to observe the efforts of our teammates in a positive perspective.

Promote team agenda:

Any person who gives more importance to his own agenda over the team's agenda is sabotaging the team's efforts. It will not only endanger their individual achievement but affect the team's ambitions as well. If we promote the team's agenda over our own personal agenda, we will help the team in its accomplishment and in turn guarantee our own achievement and growth.

Show other teammates in good light:

When you show your teammates in good light by talking good about them, acknowledging even their minor achievements, it creates a positive vibe among the other teammates. When you constantly talk good about your team everywhere to anyone, it boosts the team's image and creates a vibrant working atmosphere, which automatically ensures a better individual performance.

Be a giver not taker:

Contribute to the team always. You can only withdraw what you deposit. Relationships are exactly like a bank account. Keep depositing into that account and you will never hit a negative balance. A team member who only withdraws from an account and does not bother to deposit is bound to bounce his 'relationship cheque' one day. Every effort has to be put in to avoid this situation and the only way to do this is to build your relationship with your mates by continuously depositing good work into the team's account.

Contribute to someone else's success:
Develop an attitude to contribute to the success of someone without looking for your interest in it. If your contribution is significant in their achievement, and if you can totally ignore sharing the glories and rewards, nothing like it. This is a very unique trait one can develop and is of a class by itself. Any person who can reach up to this level is sure to reap rich dividends in the long run.

Bring energy to every encounter:
In every association and interaction you have with your team, ensure that you play a significant part in energizing the team. Play to perfection in boosting their morale and motivating them to perform to their full potential. If you can compliment even on the smallest accomplishment by a particular team member especially in the midst of his colleagues, you are adding energy to him and his colleagues. By complimenting on the work accomplished rather than the individual you skillfully promote a work culture rather than an individual getting all the attention.

Sacrifice:
On 15th August, all Indians revere this day as we celebrate our independence day. There is one person the entire world credits this day to and that is to the father of our nation, Mahatma Gandhi. He is one person who selflessly worked towards ousting the British from the Indian soil. He followed the path of non-violence, *Satyagraha*, fasting, etc., in his ordeal to get the occupying force to vacate the holy land. He was jailed, tortured and insulted. These took a heavy toll on his health, but he selflessly and untiringly

pursued his path till the British left India and India was granted freedom. He never did this to garner any positions or favours. He had a selfless attitude."

Add value:

If every team player takes the onus on themselves to bring value to the team then that team is bound to multiply its success. Add value to every encounter and be productive for the team and yourself. Imagine the reaction this would produce if each and every member learns a new skill that they put to use at their workplace. It would be stupendous; and as the team succeeds so does that individual in the team.

Admit mistakes:

We are all human beings and we are bound to err, but what is important is that we learn from those mistakes and move on. Many a times when a mistake occurs and the team is affected by it, members usually pass on the buck. Always own up to a mistake, apologise and move on. Only a strong and confident person can own up to a mistake. If you pass on the buck you are demonstrating that you are the weakest link. There is no place for a weak link in a team.

Be proactive and positively aggressive:

Proactive simply means doing things before being asked to and that is being aggressive in a positive way. When your aggressiveness is directed towards the achievement of the team, you display commitment to the team. Your proactive attitude will also boost the morale of the team and keep them motivated.

Play to win:

When you are part of a team always play to win. It is a total waste of time, energy and money if you are a silent observer or are influencing the team negatively. Abandon the attitude of 'If I cannot win, I'll not allow others to win'. This is a self-destructive attitude and a virus which will grow beyond your control and will damage your prospects in gigantic proportions. When you are already in the game, give your best shot and every time play to win.

Become predictable:

Once you become aware about the agenda of the team, you will have to demonstrate commitment of the highest level. There is no bigger an asset to a team than a dependable team player. A dependable team player would be predictable about his positive contribution to the team. His future actions will be counted in advance and accepted with confidence. If a team player can strive to achieve this position and inspire other team members to be predictable like him, then the team is definitely a winner. Be predictable like the sun — one can forecast exactly at what time it will rise and set. For centuries the sun has been committed and has been doing the function it is supposed to do. It will do so until the universe remains. As I had mentioned earlier, we get to learn a lot from Mother Nature.

Raj concluded by sharing his wisdom for that day. He said he would be going home to pick up his family and then proceed to a function they had to attend.

Raj asked me if we could do the next meeting at his Centerville restaurant. I had heard a lot about the restaurant and had also read an article in Washington Post about it. I was eager to see that place which had become a talk of the town.

I stepped out with even more enthusiasm about our next meeting.

How to improve commitments:
- Be crystal clear about your goal
- Learn to give more to your team

- Obey your mentor with respect
- Be proactive, not reactive
- Become predictable for your input to the team

My strengths:

1. _____
2. _____
3. _____
4. _____
5. _____

I want to improve:

1. _____
2. _____
3. _____
4. _____
5. _____

> *You can't cross the sea merely by standing and staring at the water.*
> **- Rabindranath Tagore**

Chapter 6

Champions aren't made in the gyms. Champions are made from something they have deep inside them — a desire, a dream, a vision.

- Muhammad Ali

Talent wins games, but teamwork and intelligence wins championships.

- Michael Jordan

To succeed in your mission, you must have single-minded devotion to your goal.

- Abdul Kalam

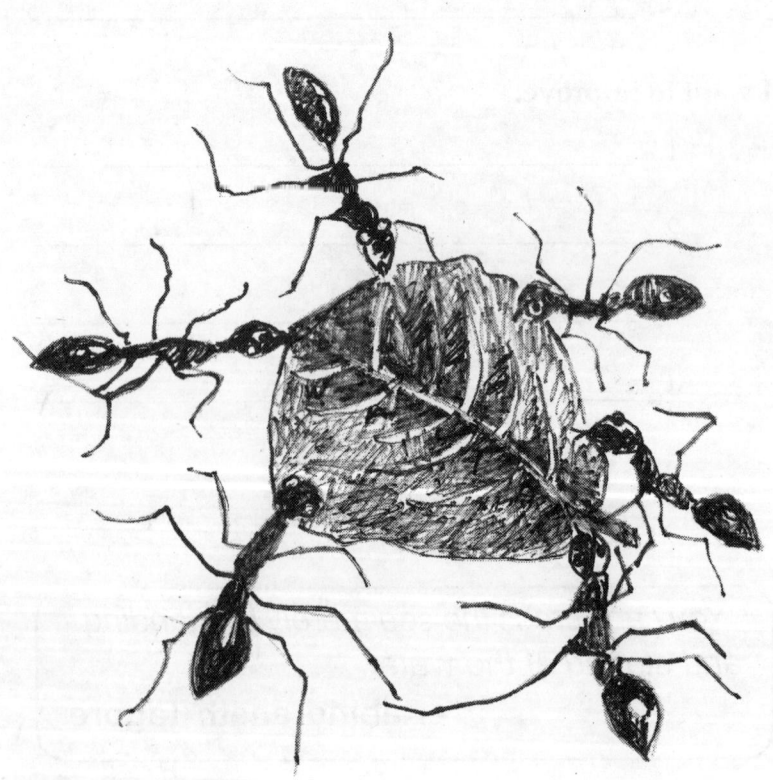

Focus on the Mission of Your Organisation

As suggested by Raj during our last meeting, I was at his Centerville restaurant in Virginia. When I walked in I could not believe my eyes. There was a typical Indian village right in front of my eyes. The entire decor gave me the feeling that I was in my village. What caught my eyes was the six-feet wide well with a rope, pulley and a steel bucket. They even had a bullock cart with huge wheels in place. The lighting too was special, camouflaged with traditional lanterns (hanging lamps). The terracotta murals on the wall, the oil paintings and every other accessory created the typical Indian village flavour. I stood transfixed looking at the Indian village before me. It indeed was a nostalgic feeling. I could not believe that I was just a few miles away from Washington DC.

Raj saw me coming in but gave me time to enjoy and feel the place. He waved at me when I looked at his direction. He was sitting with a much younger-looking gentleman and signalled me to join them.

Raj introduced me to AJ (Ajay), the manager of the restaurant. He was a charming guy and a character that you would develop an instant liking to. AJ sat for a few minutes with us and later excused himself as he had to attend to some outside work. The entire staff in the restaurant left for the guesthouse during the afternoon break leaving just Raj and me there. The staff would return by five for their evening shift and that gave us enough time to talk.

"When we bought this restaurant, we decided to give AJ the charge," Raj said.

I interrupted him and asked, "Wasn't AJ your junior most staff once?"

"Yes the same guy who asked me to get a loan and buy the first restaurant." Raj replied enthusiastically and continued his story.

"AJ is one guy with grit and determination. In spite of being the junior most guy, he showed his flair for ambition that time itself, but he had to learn many skills to give wings to his ambition. He was a good team player and was always ready to learn. He worked under Tony when we bought the second restaurant. Tony was extremely impressed with his learning skills and personally mentored him. He blossomed in the supporting atmosphere and all his hidden talent was nurtured one by one.

He had a bad beginning in USA; he was made illegal by the people who got him here and was exploited to the hilt. He escaped from their clutches and approached Tony seeking a job. He didn't know anyone as his external contacts were also restricted by his former employers. Fortunately we were looking for a guy who could remain long term with us. So I requested Anand to employ him. AJ transformed quickly and was a big help to everyone.

He was ready to change and adapt, always serving the team with a selfless attitude. He was ready to go through any challenge to learn new stuff. Because of this enthusiastic attitude, he was proactive in getting himself into the team of all our new outlets. He got involved right from the setting up stage and would be with the outlet till it began running smoothly. Later he would join other new venture of ours. By putting himself into uncomfortable situations, we knew this guy was preparing for something big. His perseverance and determination amazed both Tony and me.

So while we looked at this property, AJ suggested that we try out a typical village setup as the surrounding township had lots of Indians who had settled here some thirty or forty years back. He said we could make this into a nostalgic place for them to hang out. Moreover, it would appeal to all nationalities as we would be offering something different in the ambience and the cuisine. Both Tony and me readily agreed and signed the deal and we informed AJ that he would take care of the place."

Raj pointed towards the bullock cart and said, "AJ personally handpicked all these from different parts of India and got them shipped here. Again, who got the shipment cleared from Baltimore and personally supervised the decor. He was so focused on his vision to manage a restaurant of his own choice that he went through all the obstacles undeterred."

We have heard the story of the brick and the mansion umpteen times, but I still need to share this because there isn't another good example about the focus that is required on a mission.

The story goes this way — three masons were working with bricks and when asked what they were doing, the first one answered that he was laying the bricks. The second one answered that he was constructing a wall. The third one said that he was building a cathedral which was coming up here and soon would be a landmark.

AJ had the same attitude that of the third mason. He knew what he was building. He had a complete understanding of the mission in hand.

Visualise:

Have a crystal clear vision of a happy ending before embarking on the mission. Visualise achieving your goal. Focus on the mission all the time with single-minded concentration. Focus, focus and more focus; that is the only way you can accomplish your mission. Write down your goal and read it every day or post it on your mirror. Have you noticed how some popular brands advertise lavishly?

Sometimes when you surf television channels the same product is being advertised in all of them at the same time. The intention is simply to remind the prospects constantly of their product. 'Out of sight is out of mind' is the mantra they follow. We have to adapt that mantra seriously into our daily lives. If you let your attention slip from focusing on your mission, it would be a bigger task to bring it back to focus. So write your goal down in a place where you can look at it all times. Let it constantly keep you aware of your mission and keep motivating you every time you look at it.

Enjoy your work that needs to be done:

When a team is charged up just being there will definitely help you, but that is not what teamwork is all about. Teamwork is all about submission. Better put as, 'submit to the mission'. It is natural that all the work may not be enjoyable, but when you focus on your mission all the disliking would disappear and you would finish the work even before you realise it. Develop a liking for the work you dislike, though it is easier said than done. But if you are left with no choice and you have to do the work anyway, why not enjoy and do it."

Focus on the solution:

If we know the fruit that our hard work is going to bring, then it is easier to stick to our mission. Focusing on the solution instead of the challenges will help us stick to our mission better. There are no difficulties in this world that do not have a solution. Get out of the habit of seeing problems and negativities in every issue; instead join the club of solution finders. You and they will enjoy tackling the issue much better.

Monitor your productivity:

Keep monitoring your productivity metre periodically. Activity without productivity is a killer, and it is a vicious cycle too. You cannot have productivity without activities.

Abandon activities that are nonproductive. Focus more on activities that are fetching you results. Later, improve your style of functioning to accomplish more in a less time. Your stock value in your team will soon be at its optimum. Good team members will emulate a successful team member. Gradually, a team with its members focusing on productivity will achieve much more than those who are merely active. A proven method is to write a to-do-list first thing in the morning. At the end of the day strike out what has been accomplished and carry forward the remaining to the next day's list. By following this simple method you are definite to accomplish more every day.

Work together to win together:

To achieve stupendous performance a group needs to work together first. Winning together follows much later. When a team member values the input of his associate which enables him to work much easier and perform better, then that is a collaborative attitude. The value and appreciation other team members receive results in their own higher performance. As the overall team's performance shoots to a new high, the synergy level of the team also peaks. Any team with a renewed synergy is bound to perform better and any team performing better is bound to win. Focus on the mission of your organisation and work together to achieve it, for when we work together we win together.

Contribute every day:

Do something every day for your growth that will help you focus on the mission more positively. This could be done by doing more research in your field of work or adding skills to your profile that will help you along the way. Whatever it is or in any form your contribution may be, make sure you contribute on a daily basis so that the project succeeds. A contribution a day keeps the project alive and eventually will guarantee success. Your constant focus is a must for the success of your mission. Get addicted to it in a positive way.

Program yourself positively:

The mind plays an important role in the success of your mission. Make sure you feed only positives into it. Negativity is all around and it is often a slippery road; you need to be aware and awake all the time. If at any point of time you feel you are slipping into negative thinking, freeze that thinking immediately and replace it with an exact opposite and positive image. Program your mind positively all the time. Negativity will spread like a virus in your system at an unbelievable speed. Before it wipes out all your efforts, constantly run your anti-virus of positive thinking. It will help you focus on the mission positively."

We heard a group of people talking and both of us looked outside and saw the staff approaching the front door of the restaurant. It was almost five in the evening and the staff had started coming in after the afternoon break. By then Raj had finished sharing his thoughts and I again thanked him for choosing his new restaurant to share his wisdom this week. We both got up and walked to the car park and spent a few more moments surveying the beautiful strip mall where the restaurant was located. We had parked near the Starbucks coffee shop and the manager saw Raj walking towards his Cadillac. I saw him coming out waving from his store to have a word with Raj, and I stood there transfixed to see the charisma Raj had on people. I sat in my car looking at the Cadillac pulling out from the parking lot and slowly glide towards the exit and onto the main road. I too pulled out from the parking lot and drove to the junction that took me towards 236 West to Alexandria. As I kept driving, I felt extremely excited about the great moments I had spent listening to the success mantra from the very person who used it to succeed. I was yearning now for more and could hardly wait for the next appointment.

How to focus on your mission:
- Be crystal clear about what you want to achieve
- Break down your goal into smaller steps
- Visualise about achieving your next step
- Motivate other team members by showing them the larger picture
- Keep speaking good about the team to one and all

Points to ponder:
- How serious are you about your mission?
- Do you constantly visualise achieving your mission?
- What is your attitude and body language when you talk about your mission?
- Promote the mission to team members constantly
- Write down and post a note in your work area

My strengths:

1. _____

2. _____

3. _____

4. _____

5. _____

I want to improve:

1. _____

2. _____

3. _____

4. _____

5. _____

A team in an ordinary frame of mind will do ordinary things. In the proper emotional stage, a team will do extraordinary things. To reach this stage, a team must have a motive that has an extraordinary appeal to them.
- Knute Rockne 1888–1931

Chapter 7

> *Alone we can do so little; together we can do so much*
> — **Helen Keller**
>
> *"Individually, we are one drop. Together, we are an ocean."*
> — **Ryunosuke Satoro**
>
> *Individual commitment to a group effort —
> that is what makes a team work, a company work, a society work, a civilisation work.*
> — **Vince Lombardi**

Collaborate for Multiplying Results

Raj looked even more excited today. He had told me that this phase of his life was his most exciting and that which he personally enjoyed the most. He had put a team in place that duplicated him and multiplied his activities so that the results also multiplied by themselves, without him physically being there. Raj had given me a hint last week that he would be revealing to me about the phase where he had made the quantum leap in his profession. The phase where he had actually achieved two hundred times his potential, exactly as in the graph he had shown me during the first session. I had prepared myself, to gather the best firsthand knowledge that I had ever received, based on the principles Raj had mentioned earlier in the sessions.

Raj cleared his throat and continued sharing with me his success story.

"After witnessing the geese flying in a V formation, I kept thinking about it for quite a few days. When I was back in my room one day and relaxing, I casually picked up an Indian magazine that was lying nearby. I glanced through it and my eyes fell on an article on Maruti cars that were being manufactured in India and exported to many countries around the world. The article said that when Maruti was introduced in the early eighties in India it had just a single model — a 0.8 litre (800 cc) hatchback. Those days there were two formidable brands in the Indian market namely 'Fiat' manufactured by Premier Padmini Ltd and 'Ambassador' manufactured by Hindustan Motors. Around the late eighties Maruti entered into a collaboration with Suzuki Motors of Japan and started manufacturing two more models and improvised their own 0.8 litre (800 cc) car.

Today after two decades the story is that both Fiat and Ambassador have folded up and Maruti is the largest car manufacturer in India with over a dozen models to offer, not just within India but in the international market too. There were also reports that it was being exported to more number of countries than few other international brands. Today one can find almost all the leading brands of cars and automobiles on Indian roads. If you take the cars of the same class and pitch them against Maruti's models, either they will beat them in their looks, performance and price or one would at least give them a second glance. The article said that Maruti was not only able to survive the competition but actually beat it, simply because they collaborated with another successful car manufacturing company. The collaboration was probably enjoyed most by the staff of Maruti. It was not just the working atmosphere, the engineering skills or their increased pay packet but with time they transformed into a highly skilled workforce and better human beings, to be a better support to their family, under a new leadership.

Collaboration with a higher source is always beneficial. The law of physics says that the natural flow is always downwards. Similarly, knowledge from a more knowledgeable person flows to a lesser knowledgeable person. Likewise, money flows from the rich to the poor. When you collaborate with a person of higher calibre, contact or intelligence you always stand to benefit. Your own knowledge and stock value increases.

Collaborate for multiplying results:

When we associate with a team or when we are part of a team our net result is also in proportion to our input. Let me explain it this way. Let us assume that you work one hundred percent to your potential, and let us also assume that there are five members in your team. As all of them work to their full potential we could for example rate them as ten out of ten. Now as each of these members, who are rated ten out of ten, work together their total output would be 10 + 10 + 10 + 10 + 10 = 50. The team's output would be a total of 50 and when you divide the resultant 50 by 5 which is the total number of members in the team you get 10, the individual output. As each member's input was ten their output is also ten. Here the output is equivalent to the input. From a business standpoint you are neither making any profit nor incurring any loss, but what is safely referred to as realizing a breakeven point. When you associate you are in an agreement mode, and in agreement you only add up.

But when you are giving ten out of ten, which is one hundred percent of your performance, it is not fair to be at a breakeven; rather you should be reaping a profit. One can collaborate only when they are in an aggressive mode, and when you collaborate with this attitude you go into the multiplication mode. The passive mode is association and the aggressive mode is collaboration. This is the phase when water turns into steam. Water cannot move an engine, but steam is the power behind massive ships. It is the same changeover that happens when you shift from an agreement mode to an aggressive mode. Then you are not in the addition mentality; you shift gear to a multiplication mode because of your aggressive mentality. When the same five members of the team work aggressively the multiplication effect is 100,000 ($10 \times 10 \times 10 \times 10 \times 10 = 100,000$). And when you divide the total output of 100,000 by 5 (number of members in the team) you get 20,000. That is two hundred times your input. When you are already giving hundred percent of your potential, does it not make sense to work in a collaborative mode to multiply the results. Collaborate to not just add value to your team but to multiply that value.

Collaborate through network:

When you increase your network you become a strong and influential person yourself, may be even more powerful. If you have noticed, a rim on the wheel has spikes from the outer circle coming into the inner circle. The inner circle is supposed to be

> Collaborate to not just add value to your team but to multiply that value.

the strongest point in a rim, because of the protection and strength distributed from all sides coming into one single point at the centre. A network of friends works the same way. All the influence and strength of your friends or contacts flow into one person, which is you, making you a formidable person. In today's world everything is about whom you know and how much you know them. The more the better; the higher their position the higher you get elevated to as well. Identify whose friendship will benefit you in the long run and work a way to get into their inner circle. But beware — your approach has to be genuine and honest. If you have any inclination for manipulation, you would be bared and would lose much more than what you had bargained for. So honesty and integrity is the key here when expanding your network. See how you can help them rather than you getting helped. Focus on the benefit they will have by associating with you, not the other way. If there is something you see and notice where you could be of help, offer it without malice and anticipation. You would be amazed at the positive results this will bring in the long run.

Dare to walk up to your opponent and hug them. If you are concerned about your growth and the support of your opponent is imperative, then you have to surrender and meet up. I do not mean that you have to be manipulative. Take a look at the explosion of networking sites online. MySpace®, Facebook®, Orkut, LinkedIn® are all registering a humongous growth in membership. Even celebrities are getting on

Twitter to reach out to their fans and multiply their network and support base.

Empower others:

As I had said earlier there were quite a few investors who were in constant touch and were always on the lookout for business opportunities. I want to remind you again that these relationships were built over a period of time and there were enough opportunities along the way to prove each other's trust and integrity. Once my own restaurant started doing well, these investors were constant visitors and we would indulge in brainstorming sessions once in a while. On one such occasion one of the investor friends mentioned that there was a restaurant that was closing down due to poor management in a neighbouring town. He said that the location was good and would prove to be a good investment. I was not in a situation to invest as I was clearing my earlier loan. He proposed that he would bring in the entire finance but on a fifty-fifty basis and that I could repay him after I had completed the existing loan.

I asked for time to think it over and we met the next day to thrash out the contract part. I told him that I would have an assistant of mine running the day-to-day work at the new place, and I would visit only once in a while after the initial setting up and running was handed over. My investor friend agreed and we took over the place. As the work continued at the new place I sat with my main chef; I had trained and supported him just as I had been nurtured initially. I gave him the same offer I had been given once and a bit more. The twist was that I would not be interfering in the day-to-day matter, and he would have to handle the restaurant as if it were his own. I also agreed to pay him a percentage of the turnover every year apart from his salary. In my case there was interference at every level by the owner, and after some time it had become more of a pay back because my owner had gifted me a life in USA. So his argument was that I owed him everything making me feel like a slave at times.

I had decided then that when I would become an entrepreneur I would do exactly the opposite. I would empower and delegate, give my people the freedom and allow them to make mistakes and correct them only if they repeated it. It was in the light of my own experience that I told Tony, my main chef, that he would be in total charge of the new restaurant and would only send me monthly reports and deposit funds into the bank. Also, that I would not step into the premises if everything went smooth. We had a gentleman's agreement and both of us kept it. I was there for Tony whenever he wanted me, and after about six months of operation I never had to look into the affairs of the outlet. It did so well that in less than eighteen months' time I was able to return what was supposed to be my share of the investment along with the interest part.

Tony was extremely happy as he was able to bring his family to the US. He also bought a house of his own and started leading a blissful life. The staff working in both the restaurants for the past few years now saw the benefit of loyalty, hard work and sincerity paying rich dividends. I started getting open support from the staff of both the outlets, and with Tony's help we started nurturing talented youngsters. On our second anniversary a rich friend of mine proposed investing in a third outlet in which he was willing to finance up to fifty percent of the required funds.

I had invested in another property and found it a bit tough to shell out fifty percent of the proposed deal. With my investor friend's permission I placed the offer in front of Tony. So now there would be three partners as against the two in the previous deal. Tony took the offer with open arms, and this time Tony did the talent hunt and placement. My work was reduced substantially. Tony was there for me on every occasion before and after the deal went through; we had now become much closer."

"If I may ask how many restaurants do you own now, Raj?" I asked curiously.

"Fifteen as of now, out of which four outlets are in partnership with Tony alone."

"What about the other eleven outlets?" I was even more inquisitive.

"As you know, the first one was started independently so eight of the rest are co-owned by the chef in charge of each outlet. The second and third had different investors. All of them are debt free now and making decent profits. Once an effective team was put in place I never stepped into any place to micromanage or check on anything. They take care of the entire day-to-day operations. I do visit often and spend time with the team to let them know that I am available to them at any time. I make sure that I am there with them during their time of need.

Managers and team leaders ensure that there is a smooth flow of functions. Now with net banking, I have access to bank accounts from anywhere in the world. The statements from the outlets reach me on time. One has to sweat it out to put a good team in place. But once that job is done then you can sit back and relax."

Raj stopped to take a sip of water from the glass and then continued.

"Empowering others is something I learned during my chef days. I identified colleagues who were loyal and ambitious and helped them in whichever way I could. If they got an opportunity they would deliver and I started helping them to improve themselves on many fronts. When you are in the process of empowering others you have to be genuine. It has to be done without any ulterior motives. Because when you help someone with hidden intentions, it will most likely have a negative impact. One, because the person whom you have helped may not reciprocate the way you want them to and this will create friction amongst you; and two, as per spirituality, you should help others without expecting anything in return.

When you empower others on a consistent basis you take the focus off of you and concentrate on uplifting someone else. This has a tremendous advantage because the pressure is off from your own work and accomplishments. When you continue empowering others without realizing, your own growth occurs. As you keep sending positive vibes all the time you also start attracting positive energy in multitudes, which is essential during the growth stage.

Complement your teammates:

When you help a weak teammate improve their performance, you are completing them. You will attract people to you when you complement them, but when you try to compete with them you repel them. We need the support of every member in the team to achieve our organisation's goal as well as our individual goal. So attracting people towards you is important rather than repelling them.

Surrender your pride:

When you work with a team you have to let go of your pride. Otherwise it will create unnecessary troubles and will block your growth. It is false ego that promotes pride. Take an honest stock of the situation and realise what you are actually worth. After having understood, surrender your pride to surge forward. People love to associate with a person without pride. The chances of an ego clash among teammates are high if one harbours pride. The team suffers so does the organisation due to ego clashes among teammates. Collaboration is only possible when both parties surrender their ego and work together to achieve a bigger goal which is otherwise not possible.

> When ego comes, everything else goes. When ego goes, everything else comes. Don't drop relationships to save the ego. Instead drop the ego to save relationships.

Command respect:

You will repel people if you resort to demanding respect. You can attract people towards you by commanding respect. In your quest for becoming a good team player, an outstanding supervisor, an effective leader, a productive manager or a dynamic executive, strive to become a good human being as well. If you demand respect you will get it owing to your position but it will vanish along with your position. Your position at the most will last your working career, say a maximum of forty years. However, when you command respect it will last not only your lifetime but many times beyond that. All you need to do is look at the great leaders who command respect even after they have gone. By working on to become a good human being you will not only command respect but you will also draw people to you and that will make it easy for you to collaborate.

Create productive partnerships:

Individually we can do only so little; we need strong partnerships to make it big in life. When you choose your partner they need to take you to an altogether different high. You automatically assure growth by associating with already successful people. Be willing to undergo some trial and error in the process of finding productive partnerships. A partnership where both the involved parties benefit will sustain the test of time.

Recognise and value:

Recognise and value the input of everyone who has helped you accomplish your mission. Take a look at the thirty seconds' speech of the Oscar winners from the stage. Invariably almost everyone gives credit to the person or the teams who have helped them achieve that covetable award. Let's analyze the recent successful Hollywood movie *Avataar* by James Cameroon. He had a vision and a story line, but with a whole lot of diverse units had to understand, believe and deliver that which he had visualised. Set designers, sound recordists, visual effects technicians and various actors, animation experts and the list goes on and on. Look at the long list of names that scroll through the credits at the end of any movie. When a person gets credit and he lets the world know that there were a whole lot of people behind his win, he is not only recognising their efforts but also letting people know that their efforts will also be recognised if they collaborate with him. And that he is least interested in garnering all the credit for himself.

Also look at the recent Indian hit *Robot*. Initially many rejected the movie idea but then came forward one person who believed in the writer and director Shanker. Soon others followed and he put together a team to make a movie which has broken all commercial records in Indian movie history. During the many ceremonies held to celebrate the success of the movie *Robot*, each and every person who was part of the movie was given credit for the stupendous success of the movie.

Drive mileage out of every opportunity you encounter by recognising your colleagues' efforts. Value their contribution for your success. No incident should go unnoticed. People are hungry for recognition; feed them as much as you can. Edify and promote everyone who adds value to you. People leave a team or an organisation simply because they did not get the due recognition.

We managed to build a good team by identifying and recognising the good effort of our team members. Today I hardly step into any of my establishments with the intention of overseeing. I do visit them often and I am available for any staff at any time. Our communication is through a proper channel, but anyone can approach me fearlessly at any time. I am with my staff and the staff stands solidly with me. The bank statements do not lie and that is enough for me to check the pulse of my business. In the past fifteen years we have added about fifteen different establishments — adding one almost every year — and all these have been built through collaboration, teamwork and empowering others."

The phone rang and Raj excused himself to attend the call on his office line. He returned to say that the call was a confirmation for his 6'o clock meeting with a realtor. He revealed that with the next week's meeting he would have finally shared almost everything that helped him succeed. As we had some more time in hand today, he spoke about his upcoming projects. I was as excited to hear about them as he was to tell me about these projects.

We bid good bye with a promise to meet next Tuesday. I left his office and walked towards the metro unable to control my excitement. I was so sure that whatever he would be sharing next week would change my life as well as of the others who would get to know of it from me.

How to collaborate:
- Become a good listener
- Work aggressively
- Help others achieve their dream
- Connect with your team
- Learn to give more to the team
- Network by associating with people of higher calibre and influence

Points to ponder:
- Are you comfortable working with people of a higher calibre and intelligence?
- Do you feel happy in others' achievements?
- Are you ready to sacrifice your ego for a bigger achievement of the team?

My strengths:

1. _____
2. _____
3. _____
4. _____
5. _____

I want to improve:

1. _____
2. _____
3. _____
4. _____
5. _____

In the long history of humankind (and animal kind too) those who learned to collaborate and improvise most effectively have prevailed.

- Charles Darwin

Chapter 8

The history of the world is full of men who rose to leadership, by sheer force of self-confidence, bravery and tenacity.
- Mahatma Gandhi

A champion is someone who gets up when he can't.
- Jack Dempsey

A hero is no braver than an ordinary man, but he is braver five minutes longer.

- Waldo Emerson

Master the Never-Say-Die Attitude

Raj was to share the last of his success mantra with me today. He had said he would meet me at the corner of 14th street and Constitution Avenue and we would take a walk together. He seemed excited to show me the spot where he said he would come and sit whenever he felt low. As I crossed the street from the metro station, I saw Raj too crossing and turning to the corner of Constitution Avenue, where we had decided to meet. He was wearing a black woollen overcoat reaching up to his knee and a black and grey muffler was wrapped neatly around his neck. He was also wearing dark sunglasses. Raj looked stunning in that outfit and I admired his dressing sense. He saw me and waved at me.

It was a cold afternoon but there were no wind. The weather was bearable enough to take a walk and as we approached the Washington monument it started snowing lightly. The sidewalk had heaps of snow dumped by the snow truck from the previous day's snow. The walkway was empty and we took a right to turn into the monument park. Raj stretched his hand and let a few snowflakes fall into his palm. It was magic to see the light flakes drift and slowly drop on to his palm and melt away.

> **Snowflakes are individually very light, but rock solid when they stick together.**

"They are unbelievably light, aren't they?" Raj looked at me and said.

"Even though they are light they turn rock solid when they stick to one another. You will need a shovel to remove them from there." He pointed to the sidewalk where heaps of snow had collected which now resembled a white rock.

"I thank the almighty for making me understand the philosophy of staying together and that too early in my career." Raj looked at me and revealed.

As we took a turn again in the park it had stopped snowing and the weather cleared and everything around us looked vibrant and clear. By now we were at the foot of the giant monument.

"When I feel low and drained I come and sit here. I take a deep breath and look in that direction. I get instantly inspired and I do not know where all the energy comes from to fight back and tackle all the obstacles I am facing," said Raj.

I looked at the direction Raj was pointing. I was stumped by the view and what I saw. I was looking directly at the Lincoln memorial. Though it was a mile away from where we were standing, the imposing statue of Abraham Lincoln flashed in my mind. I had been there many times and knew how it felt to stand underneath the nineteen feet tall statue where Abraham Lincoln is sitting on a chair overlooking the Washington monument and further down is the US capitol building, all in one line. Those who have seen it would admit that it is one of the finest historic monuments in the world.

"This man takes away all my excuses," said Raj pointing towards the statue.

"An ordinary man who had just twelve months of formal schooling and a life of struggle, who faced failure after failure for over thirty long years. Through his sheer grit and determination he went on to become the president of the United States of America. Lincoln is not just revered in the United States but all over the world; an ordinary man who went on to become extraordinary through his deeds. When I look at him I have no reason to crib because I have not faced his kind of struggles and challenges nor have I failed that many number of times like him. If he could show such grit and determination and stick to his goal and work on it till he succeeded, I have no reason but to keep working at my goal. The kind of tenacity which he displayed is a lesson for the entire mankind."

Raj's eyes were moist with respect and admiration for the late president of the United States of America, Abraham Lincoln.

Mahatma Gandhi showed the same determination and never gave up until he was successful in making the British leave the Indian soil. Fight until you succeed — that is tenacity. These great men had a never-say-die attitude. And that is what I want to share with you today. Let any obstacle come your way, find a way to move ahead. Keep moving until you reach your goal. You will be tested throughout your journey to your goal; you may even consider quitting but testing times are not quitting times. That is the phase where your true character is revealed. To swim with the flow is easy, but you never realise your strength at such a time. It is only when you swim against the tide and cover the distance is when you realise how strong a person you are. The resistance you develop on the way makes you stronger than before. When you start admiring yourself on the simple feats you accomplish on the way, you would gain that confidence to face more and bigger challenges. Once you conquer your goal you will enjoy the success even more.

I asked Raj who had his eyes fixed on the Lincoln memorial once again. "Raj if you would pardon me, your story sounds more like a fairy tale. Success is not so easy. There are lots of talented people who struggle to find the right chord and they keep struggling to find success."

Raj turned towards me and put both his arms on my shoulder and looked straight into my eyes and said, "I am glad you asked me this question. We were talking all along about how to work with a team and to get the best out of your own potential."

I nodded in agreement.

"I had my share of failures and setbacks, as a matter of fact I failed miserably and looking back I guess I failed ninety five percent of the time. The success what you see is simply due to sticking it out in spite of being almost wiped out many times."

As he removed his hands from my shoulder, I asked him if he would mind sharing few of his experiences. He took a deep breath and continued.

"When someone sponsors you for your stay in America then you are at their mercy during the sponsorship period and they keep you on a tight leash. Some people are extremely harsh during the time and exploit you to the hilt. Most of the sponsors are genuine, extremely nice and honest. There are those small exceptions and Anand was one of them. During my initial employment days, for about two years, I was made to work for almost sixteen to eighteen hours a day with multiple responsibilities. He constantly kept me busy depriving me of my time to settle down or think. He made sure that I got very little time to sleep so that all I did was just work, work, and work.

I was young then and this behaviour of his did not destroy me completely. Then after about a year I decided to quit the restaurant job and take up something else where I was assured of at least the same pay. There was a convenient store nearby up for sale and the amount was manageable. I found an investor and proposed to put in ten percent so he financed the remaining amount. The store would be entirely in his name. I would only receive the pay which I was taking then and he could decide after a year about the partnership after judging my performance. I decided to put in ten percent so that I displayed seriousness in the project."

This investor was another person who appreciated my work ethics. After consulting with him I went and signed the deal for the convenient store. However, when the time came to pay the remaining amount he pulled back and said he did not want to go through the deal. I forfeited the advance amount. My entire savings till that date along with what I had borrowed to make up my ten percent of the investment was lost. It took me over an year to pay off that debt."

I had married about six months into the job, and I was eagerly waiting to get out of Anand's clutches and dreamt of freedom, but here I was deeper into debts, more misery and darkness. My wife had a small job so we managed to survive. I could not tell anyone about my situation and suffered in silence."

About six months into that major setback, I came across another opportunity. A restaurant in Alexandria, Virginia wasn't doing well. They had major trouble with the kitchen staff. The owner met me and offered me a fifty percent partnership if I took the entire responsibility of the kitchen. I asked him for some time to think and he gave me a week's time. At the first available opportunity, I discussed the offer with Tony and his assistant Mohan. We three were a force and gelled well. We were confident we could pull this off but the only hitch was our monthly drawings. We had commitments, so we expressed our idea of a minimum monthly salary and quarterly settlement of revenues. The owner agreed but asked for some more time to arrange the required funds.

We waited but did not hear from the owner and when we made enquiries we were told that he had dropped the idea. During the same time Mohan resigned and left us. After about a month we came to know that Mohan sabotaged us and hijacked the deal. He agreed to all terms of the owner and convinced him that he could run the restaurant without our help.

It was a good deal and all of us could have escaped to freedom, but that was not to be. We were quite upset but we realised that instead of focusing on negative energy we would have to continue to concentrate on our work and further prepare ourselves. We realised later on that, that was the best decision as jealousy and animosity would have attracted more negatives into our life and would have pushed us further into misery. We wished Mohan well and moved on. We did not give up and kept working the same way.

Oh I am sorry Raj I did not know you struggled so much; so it must have been easy after that," I responded.

"Well, not exactly. There were bigger challenges waiting for me. About eighteen months later from that time, Anand decided to sell the restaurant and I ended up owning it. When we bought the restaurant, remember, we had a financier who put the entire amount?"

"Yes I do remember," I said.

"About a year into the new business, half of the team rebelled with the approval of the financier and wanted to oust me from the business. There was an assistant cook who was over ambitious and was looking for easy growth and money. Tony and me knew about him, but never realised the gravity of his underground activity. He used to constantly feed wrong information to the financier to get into his good books. This we came to know during the final face off with the financier.

By the end of one year into the operation, I had repaid half the amount I owed to the financier, but he still refused to make me joint signatory in the account operations. The staff salaries then started getting delayed, and when I confronted the financier, he bluntly said that I could leave the business and he would run the restaurant with the remaining staff. I refused to leave because not only had I set up the place, I had also paid back half the investment. I asked the financier to come to the restaurant and there we

> There might be challenges at every bend; you may slip down a few steps or fall back but what matters is how high you jump back after every fall.

would settle the entire issue by scrutinising the documents to determine the ground reality.

The financier came and scrutinised the books of accounts, and they were all perfect and showed substantial growth month after month. We had the habit of maintaining perfect up-to-date records; however, he still insisted that the restaurant was not being run to its optimum and that I was not good at managing it. He said he could run it with the rest of the staff and that he was ready to return my investments and bid good bye to me. He then asked the staff who had assembled there and witnessed the heated discussion as to who wanted to continue with him. That is when the assistant cook, Robin, stepped forward and said that he cooked almost all the dishes at the restaurant and so all he needed was a few assistants and some front office guys to run the restaurant.

At this moment Tony and majority of the best staff walked over and stood behind me saying that if I was sacked then they too were quitting along with me. The financier panicked. He realised he had been misguided. Now there was a vertical split within the staff with the best of them ready to move out with me. We left the matter entirely with the financier and said we would wait for his answer and then we walked out. The restaurant was closed for a week. Meanwhile, the financier tried his best to get alternative staff to match the calibre of the staff moving out. He later realised his folly and sacked Robin and we were back. I insisted that he fire the rest of the people who had been a part of the betrayal and had openly supported Robin.

We had managed to outwit the coup, but it also gave us a feeling of the spine-chilling reality around us. For a few days we struggled to come to terms with the unfortunate events that had taken place. For me it was like crawling uphill up to the gate of freedom and getting kicked right on your head to be pushed back into a deeper and darker mess. I felt that even though I was doing everything right, I still ended up going downhill. Then as the days passed by, I saw the positive side of the coup. Had it not surfaced, I would be carrying the cancer unknowingly for a long time allowing it to grow deep and wide and it would have ended up as a major disaster.

These incidents made me strong and gave me more wisdom. When I had to reconstruct the team, this time, I purely looked for attitude rather than skills. Skills could be developed or mastered but a clean attitude and a good moral is something that comes with a person.

So from then on whenever we picked a team we were extra careful. It was like handpicking the right one from a heap of pearls to make a beautiful pearl necklace.

> Taste success at least once; you will never give up in life!

Set a target of self-improvement:

Make an agenda that you would improve yourself by so many percentages every year and year after year. Set a target which is achievable and keep progressing year after year. Never lie low or settle down. Continue to follow aggressively your yearning for growth, until your ultimate goal is realised.

Follow up and follow through:

Once you decide on your goal, put it down on paper, chalk out a plan to tackle it step by step, and follow it up with determination and perseverance. Follow up and follow through until you get to the end of the tunnel. Some of the goals may not be realised overnight. A few of your dreams may need years of follow up and follow through. Will you show that perseverance? Will you show that tenacity? Will you stand by the commitment given to yourself? If you are ready for all that, only then would you reach your target that you have set for yourself and your team.

Refuse to give up:

Thomas Edison attempted over ten thousand times before he invented the electric bulb. Earlier I used to give up easily if

I failed at something. After I came across Edison's tenacity, I took a wow that I would never give up until I succeeded, especially if I had travelled some distance with it. To my surprise I realised that I never even had to attempt ten thousand times. It is true that when the going gets tough the tough get going. Keep on attempting until the goal is achieved.

Overcome procrastination:

Procrastination is slow poison. We do not realise how slowly it eats away at our enthusiasm as we delay acting on our project in hand. It is a definite killer of your ambitions. The only solution of procrastination is to simply get up and do it immediately. It is a dangerous state of mind, so program your mind to activation mode instantly.

Think alternatives:

When you attempt and fail, try doing the same thing in different ways; that is exactly what Thomas Edison did. When asked by a journalist why was he not quitting after being proven that his idea did not work, Thomas Edison's reply was that he had not failed; he had found how it would not work in different ways.

Learn to tackle "No":

An old retired man went around trying to meet people in the search to who would buy his chicken recipe. All he had was his first cheque from social security. He often slept in his car going around the country trying to sell his chicken recipe. He heard 'No' over a thousand times and then finally he got a 'Yes' sometime after that. We would not have known Colonel Sanders or the world famous business empire Kentucky Fried Chicken if he had not mastered listening to 'no'. Colonel Sanders kept on talking to his prospects until he got a 'yes' and the rest is history better put as 'His Story'.

Most people give up when they hear a 'no'. A 'no' is nothing but an acronym for new opportunity. We are humans and we do get disturbed by a 'no', but that should be temporary and we should not allow it to program our mind negatively. We get disturbed by hearing a 'no' which actually is a 'no' to your idea, definitely not to you as a person. Refocus your mind with more positive emotions and continue your activities with more passion and vigour and you are bound to achieve your goal.

Develop willpower:

Persistence and perseverance is your willpower to keep going until you succeed. Perseverance is the willpower to keep going even if you face difficulties, obstacles or discouragement on your way to your goal. Focus on your willpower and develop or improve upon as nothing comes closer to willpower. If you develop the willpower required to sustain you until you reach your goal then that is the true 'never-say-die attitude'.

Raj took a deep breath and then looked at me with a subtle smile.

"What you term as my success is the reflection of the collective effort of my team. It is the success of my team. Whatever I am today is all because of my wonderful team. You take away my team and I am nothing." Raj said with all humbleness in his voice.

By now we were back on 14th street from the monument park and Raj said he would walk me to the metro station. As we reached the metro station I thanked him immensely for sharing his success story and his wisdom about teamwork.

Raj, I know that the mantra you mentioned is related to the restaurant business, but I believe that the same principles can be applied to any industry and by any individual.

He hugged me and we shook hands to say good bye. Raj looked into my eyes and said, "Think good... feel good... talk good... and act good. Above all respect and value your team and you will achieve your dream."

He gave a thumbs up sign and said, "All the best and always **stay motivated!**"

How to develop tenacity:
- Learn from past mistakes and do not repeat them
- Keep fighting until you reach the target — persistence pays
- Prepare so well that you do not hit any stumbling blocks
- Turn every obstacle into an opportunity
- Do not give in to negative criticism and emotional black mailing
- Stick like a stamp on an envelope until the destination is reached
- Follow up and follow through
- Taste success at least once, you will never stop the rest of your life.

Points to ponder:
- Do you agree that it is success that breeds success?
- Have you evaluated the various benefits you and others would achieve by sticking to your goal?
- How soon do you bounce back from disappointment?
- Will you still pursue what is right even if you lose all support?

    1. _____

    2. _____

    3. _____

My strengths:

1. _____

2. _____

3. _____

4. _____

5. _____

I want to improve:

1. _____

2. _____

3. _____

4. _____

5. _____

> *Success is going from failure to failure without losing enthusiasm.*
> **- Winston Churchill**